PRAISE ~~~

YOUR STORIES DON'T DEFINE YOU.
HOW YOU TELL WILL.

"There's a warmth and mysterious power in story. When shared with authenticity and with awareness for others, a sense of togetherness unites us around a virtual experience. The magic lies in not only connection but also the personal imagination and creativity that's stoked within."

> **—BRIAN SOLIS**, Digital Anthropologist, Futurist, Bestselling Author, Human Being

"Want to truly be the author of your own best life? This book can help you untangle from unhelpful stories you tell yourself, and inspire you to write better ones."

> **—MARK BOWDEN**, Bestselling Author of *Truth & Lies: What People Are Really Thinking*

"*Your Stories Don't Define You, How You Tell Them Will* is a master class for storytelling. Sarah Elkins beautifully weaves her own stories throughout the book as a vehicle for learning, painting a vivid picture of what works and why. Not only will readers finish with a deeper understanding of one of the most critical skills required in today's business environment, but they will leave with something far richer—a roadmap for creating meaningful relationships and a deeper understanding of themselves."

> **—KIMBERLY DAVIS**, Author of *Brave Leadership*

"I could barely put this book down! Sarah created an experience with every story told and each corresponding activity that made me think about the stories I had been telling myself. I felt like I was with her every step of the way on her various journeys around the world. I was delighted by the reflections on the sweet moments in her life and then relished in the simple ways she guided me to consider my own sweet moments. Read this book now! I promise you will be positively changed for the better."

—**HEATHER R. YOUNGER, JD**, Author of *The 7 Intuitive Laws of Employee Loyalty*, TEDx Speaker, International Keynote Speaker, Employee Retention Consultant and Leadership Coach

"Over the past forty years I've debriefed hundreds and hundreds of hiring managers after they've interviewed my candidates. Some big things stand out for those they liked. First, they all said the quality of the questions asked were insightful and important. Second, they said the stories the candidates told about their accomplishments were memorable, believable and impactful. Both are required to be considered a finalist for any job. Sarah's book, *Your Stories Don't Define You, How You Tell Them Will*, will teach you how to tell your own stories. And as Sarah says, how you tell them will affect your life, including how to get the job you deserve."

—**LOU ADLER**, CEO and Founder of The Adler Group, Author of Amazon Bestseller *Hire With Your Head*

"A wealth of research confirms that stories have the power to break down walls, build trust, enhance communication and strengthen relationships. Beyond just data and facts, stories enable us to express ideas, beliefs and hopes and connect with others. Stories make us human. In *Your Stories Don't Define You*, Sarah Elkins masterfully leads the reader on a journey to discover the internal messages that create one's story portfolio. From 'rockstar moments' to 'life pivot points,' each of us have stories that compose a pattern in our lives that shape who we are.

"Our stories may not be epic, but the insights, lessons and patterns within them craft a powerful internal narrative about those pivotal life experiences that create the unique tapestry that is each of us. Elkins shares her own story portfolio, giving you precisely what you need to identify, craft, and intentionally share the stories you already have that will influence how you see the world and how the world sees you. Anecdotes, real-world examples, and practical exercises are included to guide you through the process to discover your own story portfolio.

"Elkins presents storytelling as a superpower—an invaluable result of the self-reflection and introspection required to better understand ourselves, our quirks, and our strengths. When we have identified the memories and patterns that define our stories, we can tell them the way we want to: with intention, conviction, and confidence."

—**MELISSA HUGHES, PHD**, Keynote Speaker, Bestselling Author of *Happy Hour With Einstein* and *Happier Hour with Einstein: Another Round*

"As personal as experiences may be, they are also powerful interpersonal connectors. The point, though, is how stories become a springboard that propel you and your audience into the serendipitous moment when you feel you truly communicate. Sarah Elkins explores the fundamentals of interaction dynamics that make us both better storytellers and better listeners. This book gives you more than persuasion techniques: It persuades you to become persuasive."

—**MARYLENE DELBOURG-DELPHIS**, Bestselling Author of *Everybody Wants to Love Their Job*

Your Stories Don't Define You.
How You Tell Them Will.

by Sarah Elkins

ISBN 978-1-64663-111-7

Published by

 köehlerbooks™

210 60th Street
Virginia Beach, VA 23451
800-435-4811
www.koehlerbooks.com

YOUR STORIES DON'T DEFINE YOU.

HOW YOU TELL THEM WILL.

Storytelling to Connect, Entertain, and Persuade

SARAH ELKINS

VIRGINIA BEACH
CAPE CHARLES

TABLE OF CONTENTS

CHERYL SNAPP CONNER

I first "met" Sarah Elkins four years ago, I believe, through an introduction on LinkedIn. The ability for anyone—or everyone—to publish articles on LinkedIn had recently opened, and that ability had opened up an entirely new avenue for like-minded people to connect, to learn and to explore new ideas together.

Someone—I can't remember who—suggested Sarah and I should get acquainted, believing we would have much in common. Boom.

Sarah is someone who truly understands the power of communication and, in so many ways, the exponential power of using communication for good, sharing the challenges of her own work, life, the ups and downs of career, and expressing herself through the universal language of music. Sarah is someone with the courage to share not only the good experiences but the moments of greatest vulnerability—the highs, the lows—all through the lens of *the genuine desire to inspire and benefit others.*

Sarah initiated the annual No Longer Virtual NLV events to bring a select set of great minds together for their mutual enrichment and advancement in person, and out from behind the keyboards and screens that have brought us together.

But most of all, as perhaps the most defining aspect of her talents, she has put her primary focus on teaching us the power of stories—all stories, but most importantly our own stories—in defining our lives and legacies, allowing us to emphasize and document not only the *occurrences* in our lives but the *meaning* behind the events. She has become a bona fide expert in helping all within her reach to focus our attention on the stories we remember, the stories we tell, and our choice of the stories we listen to from others.

In my life and career as a communications specialist, I spend each day of my life compelling clients to understand the power of words. Sarah has masterfully taken this truth to an even higher conclusion by teaching and demonstrating the power of stories.

What we believe, what we experience, what we remember, what we choose to remember, and the way we reframe and create a story for our continual use to reinforce ourselves and for the edification of others—this is the power Sarah Elkins has captured and magnified in this book.

Due to our mutual passion for words and stories, Sarah gave me the great honor of inviting me to be the first guest of her amazing podcast on the power of stories, now well beyond a hundred episodes deep. We eventually had the chance to meet in person at an LA event where we spent an evening sharing our ideas and stories together in real life. I documented that story with a selfie photo and a single caption: "Sarah Elkins and I have met. The world is complete."

The emotion was true at the time and now carries an even greater power as we experience and document the stories of living and working in relative isolation while we combat the global pandemic of COVID-19. The stories of struggle, of sacrifice and of the human experiences that unite us carry more power now than ever before.

There is no doubt the learning, the richness and the expansion that comes from our stories is the place where Sarah Elkins's legacy lives. By reading this book and taking hold of its principles, you become a part of that legacy, too. Use that power well.

Cheryl Snapp Conner is founder and CEO of SnappConner PR and creator of Content University™. She is a speaker, author, national columnist and a specialist in PR strategy, thought leadership, and business communication.

"It's like everyone tells a story about themselves inside their own head. Always. All the time. That story makes you what you are. We build ourselves out of that story."

PATRICK ROTHFUSS, AUTHOR

WHY DO WE TELL STORIES?

As we sat at the dinner table, our younger son finished gnawing on the chicken bone and proudly held it up to show his dad and me: "Is this a Zaide bone?" We all laughed out loud, remembering with love the way my father would get every last bit of meat off a bone. If we left even a tiny bit of gristle on a lamb shoulder blade bone, it simply wasn't a "Zaide bone."

When my father died, our boys were twelve and fifteen. The only way I can imagine to keep my father's memory alive is to tell stories about him, to remind the boys of their experiences with him, and to share some of my own memories of his impact on me.

I was such a daddy's girl. I was fifteen when we were running errands together and stopped by the lumber yard; I entered my name into a random drawing and won two tickets to see Chuck Berry and Jimmy Buffett at Mile High Stadium in Denver on Father's Day. Our boys know the story of their zaide and their mom stopping for picnic sandwiches on the drive from Colorado Springs, putting down our blanket in the center of the fifty-yard line, and rocking out to those two legendary musicians. My dad told me about a fraternity party he hosted where Chuck Berry played and did the duckwalk across the stage, just as he was doing that move at the stadium thirty years later. We laughed as we smelled the joint being passed among the group behind us, and stopped for treats at a gas station on the way home.

As I share these stories of specific moments in my life with my father, I know I'm creating images in the minds of our two boys. I also know they learn a little something about their grandfather and about me every time I share one. I may even be triggering memories they have of him, based on the emotion I share when I tell them. They know their grandfather loved music, that he knew how to have fun as a dad on a date with his daughter, and they know there was something very special in the relationship between their mom and her dad.

These are priceless observations; they offer glimpses into their own future as fathers, grandfathers, and their identity as children and grandchildren.

And when I share these stories, I get the benefit of reliving those moments with my father. I get to think about how those experiences shaped who I am today, and how they contribute to my current internal messages about my confidence, independence, and adventurous spirit.

Stories make our lives richer. They provide a function of memory not served by numbers and images. Stories are our legacy, much more than any material item we leave behind. Long before there was a written story, our history was shared through storytellers. Those storytellers were honored and revered by their communities and their tribes, because they were the connection to their ancestors, their legacies, and their identities. Those stories helped our ancestors understand what was happening around them, within the context of history. Without the oral history told through stories, communities couldn't prepare for and learn for the future.

> Narrative scholars of various stripes seem to concur with the proposition that lived experience can be understood through the stories people tell about it. Stories are ways not merely of telling others about ourselves but constructing our identities, of finding purpose and meaning in our lives.[1]

---

1   Burger, 2005

To learn to tell stories well is to build a legacy with those who are in our lives for decades, months, and even moments. Communication isn't a one-way dynamic, and storytelling allows us to connect in all directions, across all barriers.

According to Carmine Gallo, author of *Talk Like Ted*, "Ideas are the currency of the twenty-first century and stories facilitate exchange of that currency: Stories illustrate, illuminate, and inspire."[2]

But telling stories isn't just about your audience; it's not just about providing a legacy for our children and grandchildren. Telling stories helps us process our memories and create our own internal narratives around them, both good and bad.

A woman with a history of abuse and neglect isn't defined by her childhood, any more than the color blue is defined by the skies of Montana. It's all about how she chooses to share her stories, with whom, and why.

From Smithsonian.com:

Scientists have "found that to build a memory that lasts hours, days or years, neurons must manufacture new proteins and expand the docks, as it were, to make the neurotransmitter traffic run more efficiently. Long-term memories must literally be built into the brain's synapses."[3]

Our memories are imperfect; ask anyone who has sat on a jury! When my siblings and I tell the same story, we tell it in completely different ways, not only because our perspectives were so different at that time, but also because each time we tell it, our memory of it actually changes. This is why the way we tell a story has such impact on how we see ourselves. If we tell a story as a victim and don't make a specific choice about lessons we might have learned from an incident, we limit the possibilities in how we see ourselves and our roles in our successes and failures.

---

2   Gallo, 2014
3   Miller, "How Our Brains Make Memories," 2010

According to Dr. Christian Jarrett, in his article "The transformational power of how you talk about your life",[4]

> Imagine that, when you were 12 years old, your family moved to the other side of the country. In your new school, you were bullied for the first time. When you reflect upon this period of your life today, do you see this as just one of many episodes in which things were going great, and then turned sour? Or do you see it as another example of a tough experience that had a happy ending—perhaps the bullying toughened you up, or led you to meet the person who became your lifelong buddy?
>
> It may not seem as if the way you tell this story, even just to yourself, would shape who you are. But it turns out that how you interpret your life, and tell its story, has profound effects on what kind of person you become.

So, how do we tell a story full of images and emotion to get the full benefit of that story on our internal messages and engage an audience when necessary?

What you focus on is what you see.

Ever notice how when you decide you are going to get a certain car, you suddenly see that particular car everywhere? Before I was pregnant for the first time, I was relatively unaware of pregnant women. But when I was pregnant, I saw women like me everywhere. It's not that suddenly that car is popular, or that more women around you are pregnant; it's that when you're focused on something specific, that's what you see.

The same thing goes for other areas of life. What you focus on is what you'll see. That's why gratitude journals work; when we begin to look for good stuff, we see good stuff. In some cases, this is called target fixation.

---

4   http://www.bbc.com/future/story/20190523-the-way-you-tell-your-life-story-shapes-your-personality

I was talking to my husband about target fixation and he said,

"Inexperienced motorcycle drivers have a tendency to focus so hard on an obstacle in front of them that they veer toward the obstacle and hit it, rather than veering away. An experienced motorcycle driver will see the obstacle and acknowledge it, but the focus will shift immediately to the potential routes of avoidance. The driver will focus on the area around the obstacle to find the alternate path."

As I jogged down the mountain behind our house a few days after that conversation, I realized that I was running like an experienced motorcycle driver; I was looking for the next step I could take, noting the rocks and sticks and other trip hazards, but not focusing on them. I was focused on where I could put my foot, not where I couldn't.

We can use that target fixation when we share a story. We can focus on the lessons of the story, the observations in it, instead of giving a specific positive or negative value to those observations. Observe the obstacles, see them, but focus on the end result.

When you are looking for the lesson in the story, the value you can take from it, you will find it. When you are looking for an excuse for a certain behavior, constraints in a situation, or the negative aspects of an experience, you'll find it.

In the stories you tell yourself and others, start to look for the lessons you can learn and patterns you can identify. Consider the perspective you have when you share a story: Are you a learner, an observer, or a victim?

There are many elements to a good story, always beginning with knowing your audience, and ending with keeping an emotional connection with them. Remember this: Your stories don't have to be epic; they have to be meaningful. In other words, the majority of the stories you share won't include celebrities, travel to faraway lands, or mortal danger. The majority of the stories you share, with the intention to connect with an audience, will be about those small moments in life that, when you look back, you realize were pivotal moments that shaped who you are today.

In this book, you'll read stories based on different situations I've encountered in my life that are intended to trigger memories for you that feel somehow similar. Included in this book is a worksheet that you will work through at the end of each chapter, beginning by identifying pivotal eras in your life, and then adding those specific, triggered stories within those eras, ultimately creating a story portfolio.

Elements of effective storytelling can be found in each story, and each story will end with questions to help you identify specific elements, absorb them, and practice them. When you've finished the book, you will have a collection of your own stories to see where some of your internal messages come from, better understand any patterns that contribute to your current obstacles in life, and practice sharing those stories to use in different situations.

*"But how could you live and
have no story to tell?"*

FYODOR DOSTOEVSKY, "WHITE NIGHTS"

CHAPTER 1

YOUR BRAIN AND THE STORIES YOU TELL

W e can actually tell our brain what to see by "priming" it. According to *Psychology Today*, cognitive priming is defined as

a nonconscious form of human memory concerned with perceptual identification of words and objects. It refers to activating particular representations or associations in memory just before carrying out an action or task. For example, a person who sees the word *yellow* will be slightly faster to recognize the word *banana.* This happens because the concepts of yellow and banana are closely associated in memory. Additionally, priming can refer to a technique in psychology that is used to train a person's memory in both positive and negative ways.[5]

---

5   https://www.psychologytoday.com/us/basics/priming

When we tell a specific story, we begin to look for evidence to support our perceptions, right or wrong, from that story. In chapter 2 you'll start to look for stories that create and color your internal messages, and in the following chapters, you'll uncover your stories in relationships and at work that were pivotal for you. Those are the stories that shaped who you are right now, the ones that create your current image of yourself.

If you're aware of how you might be priming your brain to see something specific, you may be able to shift those stories that create negative messages for you. You can look for the evidence in your more positive stories, the "rock star moments" (RSMs), to build confidence and to help you step out of your comfort zone and take calculated risks.

Another side to cognitive priming is cognitive distortions. From an article on Positive Psychology.com:

> Cognitive distortions are biased perspectives we take on ourselves and the world around us. They are irrational thoughts and beliefs that we unknowingly reinforce over time.
>
> . . .
>
> All cognitive distortions:
> - Are tendencies or patterns of thinking or believing.
> - Are false or inaccurate.
> - Have the potential to cause psychological damage.[6]

These cognitive distortions are one major reason to rethink those stories, those incidents, or conversations that shape our internal messages. When we dig into the details of the story, including the potential motivations of the other characters in our story, we can see where our perceptions might have been wrong. We can find evidence of a cognitive distortion and shift the way we tell the story.

---

6   Ackerman, 2017

From Melissa Hughes' book, *Happier Hour with Einstein*:

[L]et's dig into what is actually happening in the brain during priming. Thinking isn't a linear process; thinking is a linking process. Data doesn't simply come in through the senses and travel to various regions of the brain like stops on a bus route before finally producing a thought, emotion, or behavior. Instead, groups of neurons are continually processing numerous pieces of data simultaneously. To do this efficiently, the brain looks for patterns and associations. Those patterns and associations are the building blocks for thought.

When you share a story from your childhood that sends the message you're not very smart, you'll find more evidence along the way to prove that point. By telling the story, you're priming your brain to find a pattern of behaviors and incidents that prove you're not bright. No matter how much contradicting evidence is available to you—straight As in school, promotions at work, your family and friends telling you how smart you are, etc.—because of the way you tell the story from your childhood, the evidence is meaningless. You're only looking for evidence of being stupid.

When you find those first incidents that began your internal message of not being bright, and you begin to remember more details around the story, you can develop context around your cognitive distortion. For instance, if you retell the story but add information about the characters in your story, why they might have said what they said, or did what they did, you can choose the ending of that episode.

And when you start to choose the ending of each episode of the story that has been repeating itself in your head, you can alter your current reality to reflect a more accurate perception of yourself.

"Many stories matter. Stories have been used to dispossess and to malign. But stories can also be used to empower, and to humanize. Stories can break the dignity of a people.

But stories can also repair that broken dignity."

CHIMAMANDA NGOZI ADICHIE, AUTHOR

CHAPTER 2

PERCEPTION GAP

The perception gap is the difference between how you see yourself and how others perceive you. The gap can be wide and deep like the Grand Canyon, or it can be small like the space between you and the cheesecake in front of you. I find that the gap is generally much bigger when we're in our teen and young-adult years; as we become more comfortable in our skin, and more self-reflective, the gap shrinks. It can never be as close as the clothes on your body, because we cannot experience ourselves the way others experience us; we have too much going on in our brain that others cannot know. But if we're intentional about matching our actions and behaviors with our internal thoughts and how we want to be perceived, that gap shrinks to a manageable size. I call that being in alignment.

How do you intentionally shrink the gap and find your alignment?

Start by developing a clear vision of how you want to be perceived, in terms of your values and character, and then take consistent actions and behaviors to demonstrate those values.

Being intentional about what you share and how you share it will make a difference not only in how you're being perceived, but in how you see yourself.

What is a personal brand? According to Jeff Bezos, founder of Amazon.com, it's what people say about you when you're not in the room.

You don't always know how you're being perceived, and you cannot necessarily control that because the people around you have their own filters and experiences that color their perceptions of others. But perception is the key to good communication! Your intention doesn't matter if you are being misunderstood. All that matters is how the person in front of you perceives your communication.

Begin with your intention in how you want to be perceived, and with your ultimate goal for the conversation or message, and you'll see improved communication and improved relationships.

The "I don't care what people think" statement is great, as long as you're okay with the consequences of not caring what all people think. If you care what certain people think of you—your family, your children, anyone who can have a positive impact on your life and goals—then being intentional about your communication is critical.

That's why it's important to consider your role in a communication breakdown and the obstacles you face; you must care what certain people think of you if you want to reach life and career goals.

Authenticity

There's a lot of talk about being authentic, and keeping true to yourself is absolutely critical when defining and consistently demonstrating your values in your personal brand.

But if being authentic becomes self-limiting, you must ask yourself this question:

If I feel like I am being inauthentic when I consider trying something new, is it truly being inauthentic, or is it just out of my comfort zone?

In his outstanding TEDx talk, "The Importance of Being Inauthentic," Mark Bowden describes the four categories our brains put people into within seconds of seeing them: Friend, Enemy, Potential Mating Partner, and Indifferent. Mark is the author of multiple books about body language and its impact on how people perceive us. In his TEDx talk, he says that the majority of the people we meet immediately enter the "indifferent" category. The danger in this label is that no matter what you say, you're likely to leave without being heard, or worse, being understood.

His TEDx implores people to step out of what's comfortable and instinctual so their big ideas that deserve an audience get that audience.

> Here's the thing. If I was really authentic with you right now, and didn't use the behaviors that I've learned, and become highly skilled in order to become a good speaker—if I don't use my countermeasures to the "fight or flight" system as I'm in now, you'll see I'm not a good speaker. I'm just highly skilled in technique. In fact, if I were to be honest about this and authentic with you, and by authentic I mean that, for me, authenticity is you know what's good for you and you know what's bad for you, and you will do what's good for you, and feels right for you at an instinctual level . . . if I was being truly authentic with you, I would not show up for this. I'm not joking. That's a reality; I wake up in the morning and I go—the last thing I want to do at an instinctual, gut level is to stand in front of a bunch of people I don't know, and put out my life's work in front of them for them to criticize if they want to.
>
> This is the authentic me. If I came up close and showed you the real signals of predator, which are the real signals I want to display in front of this kind of large crowd, I guarantee you don't like me so much now, do you? I want you to have a look around you right now. That isn't a piece of rhetoric. I mean actually look around you right now, and turn and look at the back because there's lots of people here.

There's about a thousand of you here today.

Understand this:

You're designed to be indifferent to each other.

You're designed today to just hang out with the people you came with. You'll spot a few others who are like you, your tribal members. And you've met a lot of others today that triggered indifference. And you're going to meet them and you've got a brilliant, life-changing idea for you, your family, and your town, your city, your world, your universe. You've got some brilliant ideas, and they've got brilliant ideas, but you're designed to be indifferent to each other.

So I'm asking you today . . . I need you to be more inauthentic with each other today.

Because if you don't choose behaviors beyond your natural instincts, you will miss brilliant opportunities in your life.

If you don't go up to somebody today who you know at a gut level you're indifferent to, they hold nothing for you . . . and if you don't go up to them today and act and perform like they're your friend and ask them about their big idea, and act and perform like you're listening, you will miss something that is going to change your life. Act anything else but indifferent to the people around you today.[7]

In other words, if you stay in your comfort zone because it feels instinctually authentic, "you'll miss brilliant opportunities in your life."

Your comfort zone is a great place to spend time, but if you spend too much time there, you're likely to become bored, and you may even subconsciously sabotage yourself to generate excitement in your life. Stepping out of your comfort zone gives you room to grow, and if you're not growing, you're not making efforts to improve yourself and your relationships.

---

7   (Bowden, 2013)

Are you perfectly happy with every aspect of your life? If there is some level—even the tiniest bit—of underlying dissatisfaction, you can ignore it for a while. Eventually something will shift, though, and that tiny bit of dissatisfaction will become unbearable.

If you begin to address the dissatisfaction by reflecting on the cause, you'll have a choice to either address the cause or continue to ignore it. Either way, you're forced to learn and grow.

You can either be pushed out of your comfort zone or step out of it with intention.

Whatever the cause of your dissatisfaction, or if you simply have a desire to grow and improve, you must be self-aware and intentional about how your thoughts, actions, and behaviors contribute in shaping your life, and in how you're being perceived by others you care about.

Demonstrate Your Personal Brand. Create a Legacy.

When you decide how you want people to describe you when you're not around, you can choose actions and behaviors that will contribute to that legacy or reputation.

There are many times you can only use your words; there are times when demonstrating a specific value is impossible. I can tell you I'm a great cook, or a great driver, but until you've experienced my cooking or driving, you can't be sure. In cases like job interviews, sales calls, coffee with a friend, a first date, or a networking event, storytelling can be the best tool to demonstrate your values, talents, and strengths. When you tell someone you're smart or generous, you may not be believed, or worse, you may be perceived as arrogant. When you share a story that demonstrates those talents and values, you are more likely to make a true connection with the person, building trust and triggering a memory of a story that person will want to share with you.

It's not as simple as just sharing a story, though. How you share it makes a difference in how people will remember it, and whether they will associate those specific values with you and their interaction with you. A story that demonstrates your values has to be told with appropriate facial expressions, tone of voice, body language, and clarity.

Early in my junior year of college, my good friend lived in an apartment next door to a guy I went to high school with. He had graduated the year after I did, and we knew each other, but not well. One evening, my college friend asked my high school friend what I was like in high school.

"She was shy. And she was the kind of person who could have been popular, but didn't care."

That was NOT AT ALL how I saw myself in high school. I felt small, awkward, shy, and not at all popular. I had friends in all the different cliques, but never felt like part of any of them. The perception gap at that point in my life was Grand Canyon huge.

With self-reflection and the help of honest friends, you can learn more about yourself and can be more intentional about what you are putting out there, shrinking the perception gap.

If you see yourself as generous, and you want others to see you that way, what's the best way to make sure you've done what you can to align that value with how you're being perceived? Demonstrate generosity.

If you see yourself as kind, and you want others to see you that way, be kind—consistently. And when you can only use words to demonstrate those qualities you wish to demonstrate, tell the right story.

Why is it important to shrink the perception gap?

If you have a goal in mind, whether that's a new job, a promotion, growing a business, implementing your million-dollar idea, or simply improving your relationships with others, people need to trust you, believe in you and your ideas, and want to help.

When your behaviors and actions are in alignment with your values, people will want to help you reach your goals. This takes serious self-reflection and introspection. It's not that you must care what other people think; you must care what certain people think—those you care about and who can help you reach your goals.

Let's Start with Values

Here's an exercise to help you shrink the perception gaps in your life.

Think of three words you would want a person to use to describe you after an interaction. Begin with just three, the first that come to mind. Some examples: generous, funny, kind, reliable, intelligent, loving, competent, curious, resilient.

Those words translate across all aspects of your life: work, home, and friendships.

Think of it as your legacy, the top three words you would love to come to a person's mind after meeting you.

1)

2)

3)

Now, consider whether you are consistently demonstrating those values—every day—in your actions. What are some things you do, or can do? What actions and behaviors, consistently practiced, reveal those values?

1)

2)

3)

Begin with three, because starting with more than that can become too hard to apply with consistency. After you feel like you are consistently demonstrating those three, adding a few more will help shrink the perception gap even more.

This is an exercise worth doing regularly, because those words are likely to change as you experience different opportunities and relationships with others. Mine definitely did after having children, and they changed again when my father died. If you think about the words you would want people to use when you're in your twenties versus forties, you can easily see why repeating this exercise regularly is necessary!

Remember that to make these words stick, you have to demonstrate them consistently. If you want to be known as responsible and considerate, you cannot leave your dog's poop on the sidewalk or your neighbor's yard—even if no one is looking.

If you want to be known as generous, but you never have time or energy to help people, you won't be seen as generous.

If you want to be known as kind, and you want to know yourself that way, and you consistently talk behind the backs of people, or share negative comments/personal attacks with people online, you're unlikely to be described as kind. There's a disconnect here, and your brand is not aligned with your values and actions. This will most definitely create a level of dissatisfaction in your life.

As you build your story portfolio through this book, you'll see opportunities to share specific stories to demonstrate specific values.

*"There is no greater agony than
bearing an untold story inside you."*

Maya Angelou

CHAPTER 3

KNOW YOURSELF.
KNOW YOUR MOTIVATION.

There's space between finding what motivates you—or your "why," as Simon Sinek would say—and your "how" or your "what." The perception exercise in the previous chapter will help you get to your "why."

I actively avoid jumping into a trend. Maybe it's the Aries in me; when something gets wildly popular, I immediately become critical of it. Buzzwords in particular get me riled because they ruin a perfectly good word and concept by making that buzzword its very own thing, as if it could exist without the context of the situations and themes around it.

When the "why" trend began, I appreciated the focus on helping people better understand their intrinsic motivation, the "why" behind their actions and behaviors. I also appreciate, deeply, the application of finding your "why" in terms of aligning it with your work and family relationships. When faced with the question of finding my "why," I struggled for two reasons: I didn't want to jump into the trend, and I couldn't figure out the application in my daily life.

"I have to figure out my purpose."

"I'm struggling to find my 'why.'"

"I feel like I'm walking through deep sand, lost and with no purpose."

I realize now why the whole "why" thing was bugging me. Knowing your "why" doesn't necessarily inspire action, and talking about something doesn't change anything.

Distilling what you believe down to a basic, clear concept is helpful, but to find happiness and satisfaction in life, you have to find ways to apply it in your everyday actions and behaviors. You have to align your "why" with a "how" and a "what."

When you think about it, your "why" is likely pretty similar to the people you admire and spend time with.

Here's an example:

"I believe that every human has value and can contribute to our global community."

Follow that sentence with anything related to helping people find happiness or satisfaction in life, and you have a common "why." The values aren't cliché; the words just don't describe you as a unique human.

It's your "how" that is your unique value proposition.

Author of the book *Brave Leadership*, Kimberly Davis, refers to this as your "Super Objective":

> Unlike a leadership philosophy, or the way many people think of principles, purpose and values (your "why"), a Super Objective lives in action. It is always active. You cannot achieve a Super Objective without doing something.[8]

Finding My Why and My How—In Three Stories

It was a valuable couple of hours for me, and not because I was paid for them. I walked away from hosting the workshop with that rock star

---

8   Davis, *Brave Leadership*, 2018

feeling (RSF). It's that feeling when you walk away from an encounter, project, or situation knowing you nailed it. I call it RSF because I've experienced it as a musician, walking away from a performance with that euphoric high feeling, knowing you will do almost anything to feel that way again . . . soon. It's that sense that you're really good at something; you've contributed, and you're providing value to the people around you.

The following three stories are the events that helped me uncover my "how." Combined, I was finally able to see the pattern in my RSFs and RSMs. As you read these stories, think about those times you felt really good about what you did or accomplished. Consider why these experiences triggered those feelings.

You've had the experience of sharing a story only to realize the person in front of you isn't really listening because they're just biding their time until they can share their story. Your story triggered a memory for them, and they can't wait to interrupt. You've lost any indication that they're listening at all.

In a face-to-face conversation, I would discourage you from thinking about what story you can add to the one being shared. But in this case, I'm asking you to do exactly that. Throughout this book you'll read my personal stories with the intention of triggering your own!

Story 1: Workshop—Storytelling to Improve Sales

I had completed a two-hour workshop focused on the topic of storytelling to improve sales as part of a two-day retreat for a regional group of sales leaders, and I walked away with that RSF. When the workshop ended, almost everyone in the room took a moment to ask me a question, share a story, or hug me before I walked out the door.

As a group, we created space for everyone in that room to feel safe, comfortable, and curious. We shared stories that connected us, and we discussed what makes a specific personal story the right story to share, and when and how to share it. We talked about reading our audience, their facial expressions and body language, and we concluded that in sales, we have to be in it for the long haul if we want to sustain our business and the relationships we create. It was clear that sharing a personal story is one great strategy to draw out the stories of others. We also talked about the fact that business is about people, and that when someone buys from us, they're not just buying a product; they're creating a relationship with us.

Following the workshop, it took me a few hours to process what happened in that room. I couldn't shake the feeling that I had discovered—or uncovered—something about myself that I had been searching for.

Story 2: No Longer Virtual Conference

The sales workshop was two weeks before I hosted the second annual No Longer Virtual conference, or NLVDenver. Not quite the RSF I was expecting, as I decompressed in the days following NLV I found myself conflicted. I knew it was a success, and by the accounts of almost every participant, people got far more out of attending than they could have imagined. I couldn't put my finger on what, exactly, was giving me this feeling of dissatisfaction. That is, until I was sharing this vulnerability with a dear friend, and he asked me this question:

"How did you plan to define success with NLV?"

I was more than a little embarrassed. With all of my education, experience, and my incredible support network, I hadn't considered this important question at all. Well, that's not exactly true. I had considered what I wanted out of NLV, but I hadn't thought deeply about it, hadn't created any measurable desired outcomes, written it down anywhere, and hadn't been specific. As I planned the first and second events, I didn't think specifically about how to quantify the success of NLV, other than breaking even financially in the first few years.

When I considered the question, I realized that success for NLV was simply creating an environment for people to connect authentically, and to learn and grow together. And it was certainly a success if I measured it that way.

As I considered the answer to my friend's question about defining the success of the event, I realized I could let go of that dissatisfaction. I had to change my internal message about the purpose of the event to reflect what success ultimately looked like to me.

Up until a few years ago, I thought I processed information and feelings very quickly because I am great at identifying a problem, coming up with a solution, and taking action. But a few years ago, I realized that I actually process an event, conversation, or situation very slowly. It takes time for me to get a sense that I understand what happened at that event, incident, or intense conversation. By process, I mean to fully reflect on what it meant to me, the lessons I can learn from it, and how I'll apply whatever it is to future scenarios. I have to take time to understand those moments, to reflect on their impact on me. Now, years after the first NLV, I'm finally feeling like I've fully processed the experience.

Good things come in threes, I'm told, and it was the third event that finally brought me to recognize and understand my "what."

Story 3: Membership Social for the Women's Leadership Network

Each year, our local Women's Leadership Network hosts a social event and invites women from all over the community. The year I was president of the WLN, we rented out our beautiful local carousel and invited the women in our community to network, ride the carousel, drink champagne, and eat ice cream. The goal was to create buzz and recognition for our growing, thriving organization, and to encourage more women to join. We set quantitative goals to measure our success, such as attendance of nonmembers and growth in annual memberships. My personal measure of success had more to do with the environment we created as a board. We created space in our community for women to be together in a casual, fun place, to share food and drinks, and to be comfortable being themselves. The most commonly heard statement during the event and for weeks afterward was "I felt so comfortable; everyone in the room was so welcoming."

For a while, I focused on my "why" as my ability to encourage people to step out of their comfort zone and take risks they wouldn't otherwise take. Now I know that ability is a component of something less specific and more dynamic. It took me figuring out my "how" to truly define my "why." Sounds backward, right? Does it matter how you get there, as long as you get there?

This isn't an overnight lightning bolt; it has taken years of self-reflection and trial and error to come to my "why," and many pivotal conversations with people who know me, and for whom I have much respect, admiration, and gratitude.

Over the weeks following the three events described in the stories, I took time to consider what made them so successful and satisfying to me, and I saw a lifetime pattern emerge. Everything I've done successfully in my past has been part of my "what," from hosting guests in our home to helping people host events at the hotel where I was the director of sales, to facilitating groups for the Montana University System, to creating a safe place in a variety of government offices for people to share their frustrations and successes. All of my success at work and in life could be measured by the relationships I was building, and part of the success of those relationships was the space I created wherever I was sitting.

I had discovered my "how":

"I create and nurture an environment that encourages and inspires authentic connection and personal growth."

Wherever I sit, I am compelled to create an environment where people feel safe and confident to share their biggest dreams, fears, joys, and challenges. Whatever I am doing, I find my joy, my satisfaction, in creating space for people to take risks for personal and professional growth, and supporting and motivating them to take specific steps to achieve their goals.

And my "why" followed:

"I believe that relationships are the key to happiness and satisfaction in life. When we create an environment that encourages and inspires authentic communication and connection, people are more self-reflective, which contributes to improved relationships in every part of their lives."

Discovering my "how" took me to my "why."

Now what? I still had to work toward applying both of those things consistently and intentionally to be able to spend the majority of my days living my "what" and generating income.

What changed my perspective and my focus for my work and professional development was that by discovering my "how," I found my current purpose.

There's some expectation that when the lightning bolt hits, you'll suddenly and immediately be able to apply your epiphany to improve your income and happiness . . . but that's pretty unlikely. Though I still feel incredibly energized with my discovery, it has taken time to figure out how to apply my "how" to my work, and to everything else in my life. Because if you can't apply your "how" across the spectrum of your life activities, it's probably not your "how."

This epiphany came suddenly, after some major introspection and discussion with trusted friends, but the "how" itself was built over many years. When I realized this truth about my superpower, I was able to look back on years of RSFs to see the pattern.

There are so many things I've been inspired by and interested in, which is part of why finding this was such a challenge. I've been planning and hosting events since I was twelve years old when I planned a surprise birthday party for my little sister. For a little while, I had a catering business, and at one point in my career I was the director of sales at a hotel, planning and hosting events.

That was when I assumed my superpower was event planning and dove deeply into that activity.

One of my favorite projects was working with the Montana University System to build a common course-numbering system to facilitate simpler transfer of credits for students from system school to system school. I facilitated meetings of faculty and registrars for two years, and heard comments like this after every meeting: "That was the most productive meeting I've ever experienced."

That was when I decided my superpower was facilitation and dove deeply into that activity.

Our home is a place of comfort for many guests; we don't just feed people, we nourish them. Over the past twenty years, we've had many parties and events in our home, hosted musicians and music jam sessions, and provided solace and comfort to hundreds of guests.

At some point, I assumed my superpower was hospitality, and dove deeply into related activities.

With my recently uncovered "how" in mind, the pattern emerged.

I was applying this concept all along. My success in planning and hosting events, facilitating meetings, and providing a comfortable, nurturing space in our home was all a result of my superpower— my "how."

Your Turn

Think back on those times you felt like a rock star. I'm talking about specific experiences that left you walking away smiling, confident. Consider all parts of your life, from very early on, at home, at school, at work, any activity or hobby. If rock star moments don't easily come to mind, think about a time when you felt truly satisfied after completing a project, having a good conversation, or an event that left you with the "I nailed it" feeling.

There is a worksheet at the end of this book. Start to write down phrases or a few sentences to remind you of some RSMs. Try to remember what happened, who was there, and what you DID, specifically.

Take your time. It's not easy to come up with a list like this. If you are really down, it's especially hard to find those sparks of light, so you may need to ask a few people you trust to share what they believe your superpowers are, what experiences they had with you where they thought you really excelled.

Sometimes it's easier to take this activity to a journal, each evening writing down things that happened that brought you some level of satisfaction. If you're struggling with the worksheet, try beginning a satisfaction journal to note those daily or weekly RSMs. These don't have to be epic moments!

Sometimes an RSM happens in a conversation with your child or someone else close to you. It can happen when your fur baby responds to your command, or when you see the first results of your hard work in the garden in the springtime.

Next, as you develop the list (keep adding to it!), start to consider patterns. What is consistent in those experiences? The content or activity itself? The people? The responses of those around you? The impact? What is consistent about what you were providing or doing in those situations?

Find your "how" so your "why" will present itself. When your "why" is clear to you, your actions and behaviors are more likely to be in alignment with that "why," and you'll find more satisfaction in life.

It's always interesting to me when someone I meet sees or perceives something about me that I somehow missed. When I'm insulted by someone or feel defensive about something said to me, I start to ask myself questions: Why am I feeling defensive? What about that comment made me uncomfortable? Did I somehow contribute to that situation?

The best part about being self-reflective is the improvement this makes to every relationship in my life. When I am intentional about how I want to be perceived by someone I love and care about, I'm more confident in our relationship, and more confident in my ability to demonstrate that I care deeply for those people. My children, my husband, my siblings, mother, and closest friends are then more confident in our relationships; they share more of their joys and concerns with me, and our relationships deepen.

Relationships are the key to happiness and contentment in life. Ask anyone over the age of eighty if they have regrets, and they'll reveal the major regrets in life have to do with not spending enough time with loved ones, and focusing too much on work and material desires. In Bronnie Ware's book *The Top 5 Regrets of the Dying*, one of those is "I wish I had stayed in touch with my friends."

A Painful Side to Self-Reflection

I've had more than one abusive boss. Each one taught me valuable lessons, everything from learning to stand up for myself to learning when I was contributing to my own struggles.

In one particular situation, my boss was completely in over his head, and he took out his insecurities and frustrations on me. I would come home to share ridiculous stories of poor decisions and bad behavior, and sometimes seriously insulting stories about his lack of experience or education. Sharing them at home with my husband was one way I dealt with the abuse, because we could laugh about the situation and see the absurdity in it.

But one day we were at an outdoor community concert, standing around talking with friends, when I started telling some of the less-flattering stories about my boss. I was angry, seething about my treatment, and found myself sharing stories about him—not good stories.

As we walked away, my husband said, "Sarah, when you share

those stories, you aren't making yourself look good. Being insulting like that about your boss leaves a poor reflection on you."

Ouch.

I found myself getting defensive and angry. I had all kinds of reasons to share those stories; after all, they were true! But as I walked purposefully beside him, quietly seething with anger and resentment at his comment, I started to see his point. He was right. When I heard people talking behind others' backs, I didn't think much about the person being talked about, especially if I didn't know them, but I often wondered if the person sharing the gossip was also talking about me to other people.

It's the people who share dirt about others that I didn't really like spending time with, and I realized I was being that person.

Ouch again.

It was unpleasant enough to be corrected by someone I love and respect, and now I had to experience this additional discomfort of self-reflection.

So why work so hard on self-reflection? Because it makes us more aware of how we're being perceived by those we care about. Because self-reflection is the key to improving communication in all areas of life. If we don't know how we're coming across to others, we may misunderstand our struggles with the people in our lives. If we don't understand ourselves and get more comfortable in our skin, we limit our potential to be happy and satisfied in our relationships.

Your Turn

Think about the important relationships in your life, those that you consistently struggle with. Maybe it's your mother, a sibling, or your boss. Now look back toward other relationships where the struggle felt similar, relationships that ended or are also uncomfortable or you feel friction in. Do any patterns emerge? Are you misunderstood in those relationships, underestimated? Is there consistent miscommunication in those relationships?

Consider how finding your "how" and your "why" can help in your communication in those relationships. Take some time to find patterns in the relationships in your life; who were the people you struggled with? What was the situation? Were you in a good place, a confident place in your life when you had these experiences? Is it possible that you contributed to the friction? What was it about your personality and behaviors that may have created these patterns?

Life Pivot Points

Each of us experiences multiple points in our lives when we make a decision that changes our direction, a choice that completely readjusts the trajectory of our days. Sharing those stories can help people better understand where we came from, making a connection to current behavior and actions. Anything that allows another to glimpse our motivation and intent helps in communicating and persuading others to help us reach our goals.

It was the movie *Greystoke: The Legend of Tarzan, Lord of the Apes* that introduced me to the beauty of Australian landscapes. As I left the theater, I decided that someday soon I'd spend time exploring that continent. There are very few times I can pinpoint in my life when I really wanted something. Most of my days are spent enjoying the moment, taking whatever opportunities drop into my lap. Once in a while, though, I have an "aha" moment that takes my breath away and motivates me in a way that wakes me up in the morning, full of energy and enthusiasm. When I discover I really want something, I make it happen.

That movie inspired me to apply to participate in the first study-abroad program Colorado State University collaborated on with the University of Queensland in Brisbane, Australia, to host. The program was limited to a small number of students, and I was only a sophomore, competing against juniors and seniors for my spot. I needed references from professors, a transcript, and an essay to explain why I wanted to go. My GPA was less than impressive, so my references and essay had to really stand out to get me into the program.

Getting accepted, though, was only one small part of getting myself to Australia that semester. The cost was way out of my price range. As an exchange program, tuition was the same as I would have paid for CSU; the cost of housing and transportation, though, was significant for a hungry college student. I had ten weeks of the summer to make enough money to pay my aunt back for the airline ticket and program deposit, and to save enough money to pay for housing and fees for the semester.

I worked two nearly full-time jobs all summer long and scraped together just enough for the trip.

That experience changed my perspective forever. Studying in Australia, and then hitchhiking through New Zealand by myself for two weeks on my way back to Colorado, not only gave me the travel bug; those stories changed everything about how I saw the world and how I saw my place in it. Pivot.

Your Story Portfolio

In the back of this book, you'll see a worksheet labeled *Story Portfolio*. After each chapter of the book, you'll be asked to fill in a section of that worksheet. When you've completed the worksheet, you'll have a story portfolio to continue to add to so you'll remember specific stories to share at appropriate times, in front of appropriate audiences.

It may take time for you to remember pieces of your life in this way and for details to take shape. As you fill in cells of the worksheet, use short phrases or key words to remind yourself of the stories you'll want to remember in greater detail later.

*"Stories have to be told or they die,
and when they die, we can't remember who we
are or why we're here."*

SUE MONK KIDD, AUTHOR

CHAPTER 4

THE INTERNAL STORIES
THAT SHAPE US

E very time we share a story, an experience we had, we are processing the experience again in a slightly different way. Because our memories aren't reliably accurate, our stories change in subtle ways when we share them.

In my experience, many of our small, less-epic experiences are the ones we can point to as pivot points in our lives. We are more likely to be able to point to a specific conversation we had with someone as a turning point than an epic story about a celebrity sighting or near-death experience. I can look back at a specific conversation I had with my mother shortly after my first son was born and realize that was the moment my priorities had dramatically shifted. My career, though important, would at that point take a back seat to my child and personal life.

I didn't know the shift occurred in that moment; it was only when I told the story years later that I was able to pinpoint it. I know there were many details in the previous weeks that led to the pivot point, that it was more like a dimmer switch coming on than an

SARAH ELKINS   29

immediate toggle, but it was that conversation that turned on the light completely.

The bigger, more traumatic and dramatic experiences usually take a lot more time to process, and we may overestimate their long-term importance at the moment we're experiencing them. Individual experiences of hunger, for instance, have had a bigger impact on my worldview and my self-reflection than my epic journey hitchhiking through New Zealand.

From *A Fly Rod of Your Own* by John Gierach:

There are few broad strokes in fly fishing. It's all specific details strung together in a specific order; too many details to think about, really, but over time you wear neural pathways and that process resolves itself into something like instinct. This happens gradually and comes from nothing but repetition. There are no shortcuts, and the hunt for shortcuts only distracts you from the business of letting the craft become second nature.

Just as in fly fishing, our internal messages aren't created in a broad stroke, a single experience, or one part of our lives that shapes us. Internal messages are created in specific details, or stories, strung together over the course of time. When we share certain stories, especially the ones we share often, we're creating and adjusting the neural pathways to confirm whatever we thought of ourselves as a result of those stories.

Being able to look back and pinpoint specific incidents within those pivotal times in our lives helps us better understand where the messages came from, rather than giving it a larger label of "when I was six," or "when my father was dying."

I've read the phrase "Stop telling yourself the story that you're not good enough" a handful of times, but "you're not good enough" is not a story; it's a label, a judgment. If you want to stop telling yourself you're not good enough, try finding the pivot points—the experiences—in your life that gave you that label. Once you find a few of those events, those stories that point to a pattern in your life, you can dig into them for more clues about why the main characters behaved in the way you remember them. Those main characters can be friends, family, or even total strangers, and YOU, of course.

As you put together your story portfolio in the back of this book, you will identify some of those patterns, and then you get to choose whether they are positive or negative, and adjust the stories that you've been telling yourself, those labels you've given yourself, like "you're not good enough."

As you read through the stories in the book, I'm asking you to stop throughout, pay attention to the details of the stories that come into your memory, and really think about the stories in your life that feel similar, familiar.

If you need to, write down phrases or descriptive words in the margins to remind you of the details of your stories so you can add them to your portfolio later.

Internal Messages, Part 1

I walked home from the bus stop, ran into the house in an attempt to avoid talking to my mother, slammed my bedroom door, and started sobbing into my pillow. This wasn't the first time that year; it was an almost everyday occurrence. I was tiny for my age and looked a lot younger than my peers. At the same time, I was intensely boy-crazy; almost every diary entry had a story about a boy I liked, how I might appear to boys, or what a boy might have said to me (or not).

That day at school I had been talking to my best friend:

"I think he might like me! I was walking by him in the cafeteria and he smiled at me! You know I've liked Adam for the whole year!"

And she answered:

"I don't know why he'd like you, Sarah. You're not very pretty."

BOOM.

My world exploded. I took every word she said to heart; after all, she was my best friend. It was seventh grade, a year of intense emotional and hormonal shifts, and the creation of deeply ingrained memories. That moment was captured in my teenage brain, creating a neural pathway that would be nearly impossible to reroute. "You're not very pretty."

Don't even get me started about why being pretty was so important. This was the early 1980s, with big hair, *Grease* (the film with John Travolta and Olivia Newton-John, famous for her transformation from sweet girl next door to hot biker chick), and Calvin Klein jeans (Brooke Shields: "Nothing gets between me and my Calvins"). Every pop culture reference was related somehow to being attractive to boys, to some version of the Cinderella story, from total dork to stunning beauty with the simple addition of contact lenses and some Jordache jeans. In the '80s, the secret to a girl's success was to be pretty.

When my mom was ready to face her sobbing thirteen-year-old (again), she sat on the side of my bed and asked what had happened. Somehow between sobs, I managed to tell her.

"But, Sarah, you're beautiful! She's wrong! And why would she say something so mean?"

Nothing my mom could say brought me comfort. After all, of course my mom thought I was beautiful; that was her job.

A couple of hours later, she convinced me to join our family for dinner. With red, swollen eyes, I sat at the table, head down, sullen. My mother said, "Sarah, tell your dad what happened with Sheri today."

I hesitated for a moment, took a deep breath, and then shared the story. I'm sure in my seventh-grade mind, I had an idea of what I needed to hear from my dad and older brother—that Sheri was wrong, and that they thought I was pretty.

They didn't say that. They burst out laughing. They looked at each other and laughed so hard and so loudly that I was stunned. I couldn't wrap my head around that reaction. Tears came so fast and so hard that I could barely breathe. I ran from the table, nearly knocking my chair over, and melted down in my bedroom . . . again.

Looking back now, I can imagine why they were laughing: It was simply absurd. They were laughing at the absurdity of my BEST FRIEND saying something so cruel. I can't help but smirk when I think about saying that out loud!

But they didn't SAY that. They laughed. They didn't say what I needed to hear at the moment I needed to hear it. Maybe later in the evening my dad said something about my being pretty, but the damage was done, and I have no memory of the rest of that dinner conversation. My internal message was dramatically shifted, and for years I carried that around with me. *I'm not very pretty.* It wasn't until my freshman year of college that I finally addressed it and started to shift that message. I had to have plenty of evidence that a) she was wrong, or b) it didn't matter. But it still took time and intention to shift the message.

Your Turn

What is one element of this story that resonated with you? Was it the characters? The pacing? What, if any, memories did this story trigger for you?

Toward the back of the book, go to the first worksheet labeled *Story Portfolio*, and write a word or phrase that signifies a pivotal time in your life. My example is seventh grade. If you have an earlier memory of a pivotal time, write that down. One of my coaching clients remembered she was in third grade when her house burned down, and her family survived but lost everything they owned: family pictures, books, furniture, clothes, etc. They got out of the house with only the pajamas they were wearing when the fire started. In her first era on her story portfolio, she wrote, *Third grade.*

Now, in the cell beneath that first era, think about a specific incident that occurred in that time period. It can be an accident, a conversation, an adventure; choose a specific event that you remember in great detail. Write a phrase or a couple of sentences to remind you of the people involved, where you were, and how you felt. Any dialogue you can remember will be helpful. There's no need to write out the story; you just need something to bring those memories back so you can see if they were part of a pattern.

If you can think of additional specific events or conversations during that era, write them down as *Stories 2, 3*, etc.

Here's another internal message story for you. Read it to jog your memory about an incident that feels familiar or similar.

Internal Messages, Part 2

When I was in college, I drove a gold VW Super Beetle. There was always something going wrong with that car, and I learned a lot about how to fix it myself, because I never had much money. I have vivid memories of digging through my car and shining a flashlight under the seats to find change to buy ramen noodles. Memories of that car encapsulate a lot of the struggle and growth of that time in my life; some of those memories are pretty intense, and until I was in my early thirties, I didn't consider how they impacted who I am and how I think about myself and the world around me.

The subtler, funny stories that I was able to share shortly after they happened had an impact on me pretty quickly, and I learned lessons by sharing those stories with friends within a few days or weeks of the event.

For instance, I learned that being underestimated in an initial interaction with someone could actually benefit me. Up until this particular interaction, being underestimated was a huge frustration in my life. Being small in stature and looking much younger than my years contributed to a consistent perception by strangers; they made assumptions about me, my age, and my competence.

▲▲▲

My accelerator pedal dropped to the floor when the light turned green and I tried to move forward.

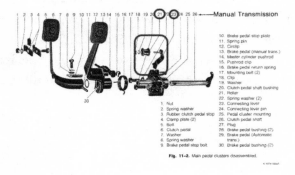

Fig. 11-2. Main pedal clusters disassembled.

Reaching down while horns were honking behind me, I tried to pull the pedal back up to rest on the connecting lever/roller. The connecting lever had disappeared. After a full cycle of green to red, and then back to green again, and some horn honking, the woman in the car behind me ran up to my window and asked if she could gently push my car with her car into the driveway to the right of the light, where there happened to be a garage with a mechanic on site. I nodded yes, please!

When my car was safely parked, the woman pulled up next to me to see if she could help. I got out of the car, dressed in a white tuxedo shirt, black miniskirt and pumps, ready to work a cocktail shift at a fancy restaurant and bar in town. The woman offered to take me to work after I spoke with the mechanic, so she was there, watching while I spoke with the mechanic.

He came out to take a look—I saw his stomach first, then his beard as he came out of the garage. He was every stereotype you can imagine: large, filthy, and with suspenders holding up his pants below his belly. He took one look at me, and I could feel the target he thought he saw on my forehead. The car was still running when he opened the trunk; it was a '74 Super Beetle with the engine in the back. The mechanic squatted down next to the car and looked at the engine.

I told him, "The throttle cable snapped." He stared at me. Then he stared at the engine again. I said, "The throttle cable snapped and I need to get to work. I'm going to be late for work." Being late was not acceptable to my supervisor, and my anxiety rose as he stared at the engine.

He looked at me. He stared at the engine. Then he pulled on the throttle toggle to rev the engine. He said, "Let's just take a look here." I said it again: "The throttle cable snapped; the problem is NOT the engine!"

He pulled on the throttle toggle again and revved the engine, ignoring me. "Hmmmm . . ."

I lost my temper. I was frustrated, hot, and worried about being late for work. I used my hip to push him out of the way (I didn't want to touch him with anything that wasn't black already), reached toward the throttle, and started to pull the accelerator cable from that end. On an original VW bug, the throttle cable snakes through the undercarriage of the car, then pops up into the driver's-side floor, where it connects with a pin coming out of the right side where the pedal is. The pedal sits on top of the pin. Yes, that pin that disappeared under the gas pedal. I pulled the cable, and pulled, and pulled until the sheared end popped out, about twelve inches of it hanging from my fingers.

I slapped the end of the cable on the mechanic's chest as I looked him straight in the eyes:

"The [slap] throttle [slap] cable [slap] snapped [slap]. I need you to get a new cable from Scott at Foreign Auto Parts downtown, put the car up on the lift, and snake it back into the pin. It should take about twenty minutes and the cable should cost about $15. I'll pay you $50 to do this. It's all I can afford. I'll pick it up tomorrow morning around 10. Okay?"

He nodded, silent. I got into the car with the woman who rescued me. I was shaking with anger and frustration. I couldn't afford this. Rent was due in a few days. I was near tears when the woman turned to look at me, put her hand on my arm, and started laughing, a big, deep belly laugh. She was laughing so hard she had tears in her eyes.

"I've never seen anything like that before in my life. That was absolutely the best! Did you see the look on his face? He was in total shock. He completely underestimated you."

She was laughing so hard that I couldn't stay angry. I started to laugh with her. As I got out of her car to go to work, I told her how much I appreciated her help. It took everything in me not to burst into tears of gratitude. She reached out and put $20 in my hand. When I told her I couldn't take the money after all she'd already done, she laughed again and said $20 was the least she could pay for that experience. "It's worth the price of admission!"

I couldn't tell the story when I got to work. Not only was I still angry and needing to get right to work, I was worried about the cost and my upcoming rent payment. It wasn't until a few days later that I remembered to share the experience with a friend, and I started to realize what a benefit it was that the mechanic had underestimated me. Because of his first impression, he was ready to take full advantage of the situation. But my response, my attitude, and my demands in how to fix the problem and what he could reasonably charge me for the repair had him scrambling to manage the disconnect between who he thought I was, and who I was proving to be.

I wasn't laughing when I told my friend the story; I was still angry at being underestimated, and having to pay for a repair I couldn't afford. My lesson wasn't clear yet, and I hadn't gotten to the point that I could see the humor in it. But when I got to the part about slapping the end of the cable on the chest of the mechanic, my friend burst out laughing. And that's when I suddenly saw the humor—because of her reaction.

She asked me what it was like when I went to pick up my car the next day. I had to think about it because it seemed anticlimactic to me. The mechanic met me at the door, told me the car was fixed, and that he wasn't going to charge me for the labor because it only took him a few minutes. The total bill was $20, which was the cost of the cable. He smiled as I handed him the $20 gift I had received from the woman who helped me the evening before.

Recap

What internal messages were created as a result of this experience? The first time I told the story to a friend, I wasn't laughing. I told it as a victim, a victim with an unreliable car who was very nearly taken advantage of by an unethical car mechanic. An internal message took shape: People underestimate me.

Carl Jung talks about the space we have between a stimulant and a response. He would say that my internal message was neither good nor bad, that it was neutral, and that I gave that message its value.

If you think about it in that way, you can choose how to use it. It took me a long time to realize that there are many times when being underestimated can give you a serious edge. It's much easier to WOW someone who has underestimated you, and in competition, people may be complacent because they don't know your capabilities. I have taken advantage of that internal message a lot over the years, because I see it as positive more often than negative.

Now, think about the telling of the story and what made it interesting to you. Did you notice I wasn't necessarily the hero? Think about the other characters in my story, the roles they played and the character development you experienced in just that short time. When you tell your stories, include the other characters to give depth, and to avoid the story being all about you.

Your Turn

Think about your internal messages that continue to swirl in your mind, and write them down here:

Example: People underestimate me.

Internal message 1:

_____

Internal message 2:

_____

Internal message 3:

_____

What memories did the two stories trigger for you? Did you remember a label you gave yourself as a result of a specific incident?

Look at what you wrote down for each internal message. Can you identify a specific incident or conversation that contributed to that message? Can you identify a recent experience when that message came into your consciousness and made you hesitate to do or say something?

Go back to your story portfolio to add the story you remembered as you read this one. Is it in the same era as the first story? Or do you need to add another era to your story portfolio?

Again, write a phrase or a couple of sentences to remind you of the people involved, where you were, and how you felt. Do you remember any dialogue? Something specific someone said to you? There's no need to write out the story; you just need something to bring those memories back so you can see if they were part of a pattern.

What was the context of the story you remembered? Who was there? Where were you standing or sitting? Try to remember the details of the environment so you have a strong, visual memory of that specific incident.

Now, think about the people involved. As an example from the first story in this chapter, I would think about my "best friend" who told me I wasn't pretty. Considering the negative, long-term consequence of that story, it's strange that I have some fond memories of spending time with her at our homes and at school, a couple of really fun school projects we completed together, and only one other time she said something hurtful to me. When I consider why she said those hurtful words to me, "Sarah, you're not very pretty," I put that comment into context with the rest of what I know about her now, and my perspective shifts.

She was really tall and very skinny in seventh grade. Some boys called her Spider as a nickname because of her long, skinny legs. She had braces and had just traded her thick glasses for contact lenses. As I look at her from this perspective, I realize how self-conscious she must have been. It's so obvious now that she was projecting her self-consciousness and insecurity onto me. It's obvious now, so many years later, that she might have been envious of my petite frame, my lack of glasses and braces.

When I tell this story now, I add those aspects of my bully, that girl who shifted my internal messages so significantly in a negative way, and I start to live in that reality. I can tell that story now with a different message: It wasn't about me at all. Her comment no longer reflects my current reality.

When one of those stories pops into your head, one that maybe was painful and impacted your confidence, dig more deeply into it to better understand the context of the behavior of the people involved so you can, in a way, rewrite the story.

In the story portfolio, be sure to add words and phrases to describe the reality behind the experience in terms of the other characters involved. What was their likely internal message in that moment? What might have happened to them to behave that way? Is it possible they were projecting their own issues onto you? Are you doing that to anyone else? Did you in the past?

Self-reflection to understand where your internal messages started and why they continued, based on other stories and patterns, is a great way to address them. The next step is to reflect on whether you are continuing those patterns with people in your life. Are you projecting your insecurities on your children, your friends, or your employees?

Look back at the personal brand worksheet: Is your behavior consistently demonstrating those value words?

In the next chapter, I'll demonstrate how I process experiences after the fact. Some other words people use to describe this activity are to "absorb it," or to "develop their thoughts about it." When we take time to process our experiences, we start to understand how those situations or events impact who we are and how we see the world before they create damaging internal messages.

"The purpose of a storyteller is not to tell you how to think, but to give you questions to think upon."

CHAPTER 5

STORIES HELP US
PROCESS EXPERIENCES

I'm decisive, often appear impulsive, and am usually extremely present, noticing all kinds of small, typically forgettable details of a moment. I used to think that meant I processed things quickly, and that's why I'm able to make (mostly) good decisions very quickly and intuitively.

By "process," I mean the activity of reviewing the details of an experience to see which pieces were particularly memorable, what impact they might have on me and a given situation, and how specific parts of the experience might have long-term effects on me, my thinking, my relationships, and my future. Some people tend to do too much processing of an experience; they turn a conversation or event over and over in their head, creating a barrage of thoughts around it that aren't particularly useful.

For instance, following a difficult conversation with someone, or a conversation with someone you're not particularly comfortable with, you may find yourself falling down a rabbit hole of thoughts:

"Did I say something offensive?" "I shouldn't have said_____."
"She must think I'm_____." "When he said _____, I should have
said_____."

Sound familiar?

This is one form of processing, and rarely a useful one. But if you
take time to talk through this scenario with someone you trust, you
might find some comfort and insight about it.

At this point in my life, I've started simply asking the person to
clarify anything I'm questioning about the conversation, rather than
spending time in my head trying to figure out something I cannot
possibly know without asking what that person was thinking, whether I
insulted them, or what they wanted to accomplish in the conversation.

Processing an experience is the key to being self-reflective, to
being proactive in your growth and learning from every situation.

When I take a trip, whether it's leaving town to spend a long
weekend in a cabin in the mountains, or a two-week trip to Europe, I
know that each experience has the potential for learning opportunities
and personal growth. How did I respond when something didn't go
as planned? What was my reaction to something truly extraordinary
I witnessed? Did I notice small, beautiful details of things or people
around me? Was I present and aware of my surroundings and my
impact on the people and world around me?

Now that I know I process experiences slowly, over time, I try to
give myself the time I need to think about important experiences, but
not immediately following them. I've found that my more intentional
or external (sharing with someone) processing is best when I wait a few
days, or even a few weeks, before I start to talk about what happened.

Processing an experience is never a simple action, and each
person processes memories differently. Choosing the person or
people to help you process an experience is critical. The people
I choose are the ones I know will ask insightful questions to jog
my memory and dig into specific incidents that have deep, broad
consequences and application in terms of personal development.

As you read the next series of stories, let your mind wander to your experiences of sharing stories with people who not only were open and interested in listening to them, but also asked questions that made you think about your stories a little differently. Again, write yourself notes in the margins when a character feels familiar to you, or part of the story stands out and jogs one of your own memories.

Processing, Part 1

Freshman year of college, Colorado State University, Newsome Hall

The food was horrible. I had the two-per-day meal plan, and by the end of the first month, I had lost a few pounds. It took me a few weeks to get into a routine, and I discovered tricks to use to get the food I needed to sustain myself. Some mornings I'd grab a brown paper lunch bag and slip an entire sleeve of bagels into it. Then I'd put a handful of cream cheese blister packs and a Ziploc bag of tomato slices into the bag. I'd bring the bag up to my dorm room where I had a mini refrigerator and toaster oven, and have breakfast and lunch in my room, where I could take my time and not deal with the smells and uncomfortable social setting of the cafeteria. Many are surprised to hear that I was pretty shy as a child and young adult, and walking into the cafeteria to eat by myself was seriously unpleasant.

One evening as I sat down to study, I realized I was hungry enough—and lonely enough—to brave the cafeteria and see if maybe I'd meet someone. You know those horror films where a person is walking down a long, narrow corridor, and the hallway just seems to get longer, no matter how many steps the person takes? That's how it felt as I crossed the cafeteria to the buffet line, and then turned with my tray to find a place to sit. Being a child of the '80s, I had images of bullies tipping my tray to spill my food, sticking out a leg to trip me as I walked by, or a tableful of students standing up to leave as I sat down. You could say I had a little drama going on in my head—and that I watched too many John Cusack films.

I saw a girl sitting by herself, and walked over to sit across from her.

"Do you mind if I sit here?"

"Nope, not at all! I'm Connie!"

We exchanged pleasantries, and I felt totally comfortable within just a few minutes. She was so easy to sit with. Not too bubbly and over-the-top sweet; she had a calm presence that immediately put me at ease.

I can't remember exactly what started the Monty Python quotes across the table; what I do remember is laughing so hard that tears streamed from my eyes. We must have recited thirty minutes of the movie *The Meaning of Life* that night, and we were loud enough to have caught the attention of a few boys nearby. I barely noticed them shifting to sit closer to us to listen in.

"So," Connie said to me, "tomorrow, same time, same place?"

Not fifteen minutes into our next dinner together, we started up again, this time quoting some of the most famous skits from *Monty Python's Flying Circus*. As we launched into the skits, I noticed a handful of boys looking over and chuckling. A few came to our table and asked to sit down. We were all laughing, accidentally snorting food through our noses, and getting loud. An employee had to come to our table and ask us to quiet down.

One of the boys invited us to join them to watch *The Holy Grail* that Friday night and shared their dorm room number. These were seriously nice guys, the kind of guys who immediately become like older brothers, protective and kind. We ended up spending a lot of time with them that year.

About a month into our time together, Connie and I got into a deep conversation after dinner in her dorm room. She knew I struggled with confidence and wanted to know why.

"What happened to you, Sarah? I just don't understand this about you."

I told her about my experience in seventh grade, how my best friend told me I wasn't very pretty. And then I shared what I believed to be the confirmation at our family dinner.

"Wait a minute. You thought that because your dad and brother didn't say you're pretty, that they believed you aren't? Isn't that kind of silly?

"And worse, you believed her?

"Sarah, let's pretend for a minute that she was right. What motive would she have for saying that to you? Really think about this. What was she going through in her life that would have made her say that to her friend?

"If someone doesn't like you because they don't think you're pretty, why would you bother with them? Pretty isn't everything. You're funny, you're caring and generous, you're smart, and you know almost every line from Monty Python's *The Meaning of Life*. What you want in your life is people who love you for those things, not because you're pretty."

Your Turn

Connie helped me process the story, the experience that shaped my confidence in seventh grade, by asking me questions that made me think about the "why" behind my friend's behavior, and the response of my father and brother that night at the dinner table. She helped me think about the entire situation from a completely different perspective, one that wasn't really about me at all.

When we tell a story, we create arbitrary constraints around why we did certain things. Instead of the constraint I created—"I'm not very pretty because my friend told me I'm not"—and then finding all the evidence I needed to support that—I didn't have a boyfriend, I was too petite, my hair was too thin and straight, etc.—I was able to shift the focus from a constraint I created to being open to other possibilities. By processing an experience with someone who will ask the right questions, we can remove those constraints to learn other reasons something might have happened, and to consider what we might do next time.

What is an element of this story that resonated with you?

Did it trigger memories for you? Did the descriptions of the environment where the story took place take you back to a similar situation?

Think about a time when talking about an experience weeks or years later made a difference in how you remembered it, as opposed to trying to tell someone the story just a few days following an event. What changed in your perception of the experience?

Next to the cell on the story portfolio worksheet where you entered your first pivotal life era, enter a phrase or code to represent another pivotal life era. For example: First Year out of High School.

Now, in the cell beneath that second era, think about a specific incident that occurred in that time period. It can be an accident, a conversation, an adventure; choose a specific event that you remember in great detail.

Processing, Part 2

I couldn't believe it was happening. My husband and I had been invited to perform with a jazz quartet at two venues in Southern France, and we were on our way to Paris, the first part of the trip. It was pretty uneventful; Bob was able to get his guitar onto every flight as a carry-on, so his stress level had dropped dramatically.

We arrived in Paris, got a cab to a hotel for one night, checked in, and then headed out to explore the neighborhood. After a pretty restless night, we got up, packed, and took a cab to a huge train station. We took the train to Bordeaux, rented a car, spent the night there, and then left the next day for our primary destination, Bilhères, France, high in the Pyrenees Mountains.

The innkeepers were full of joy and generosity; we were there to play for them. It was the tenth-anniversary celebration of their ownership of the inn and of having live music there multiple times each year for the benefit of the entire valley. They brought in musicians from all over the world to stay and play, eat, and explore that part of the world. We were treated like royalty.

Our American saxophone player was close with the owners, and they were thrilled to have him come back again, this time with a vocalist and guitar player. He had made connections with regional musicians over the years, and a bass player from previous years was scheduled to arrive on Friday at around lunchtime, so we could practice together before the performance on Saturday night.

It was 3:30 on Friday, and we hadn't heard from him. Our band leader called from the phone in the lobby, the innkeeper standing by to help.

"We just finished a short practice here, and were wondering when you'd get here so we can plan our set . . . Oh. I see. Is there a chance you could come up tomorrow, then? Okay. Bye."

"He's not coming, Jean Louis—do you know a local bass player that could sit in with us?"

I must have lost color in my face, because Jean Louis's wife, Odille, walked in just then and asked what was wrong.

"Yes! Marco would be GREAT! Let's call him to see if he's available."

After a few minutes chatting with Marco, we saw some visible relief in the face of our band leader, the saxophone player.

"Marco is available tomorrow. He'll come over in the morning at 10 to practice with us. I'm going to see him playing tonight with his regular band, so I'll get a chance to hear him."

Late that evening, I received a text from our friend:

"Marco is great! We are going to be just fine. I sat in with him and his band for a set; this will work."

We practiced with Marco for a couple of hours Saturday morning, took a break for lunch, and while my husband continued to practice by himself, I took a walk around the village.

In less than fifteen hours, we went from total panic to a crazy kind of calm.

At the sound check that evening, we met the Tahitian dancers, drummer, and vocalist who would take the stage first, and the incredible band who were scheduled to play after us, playing regional traditional music in their local languages, with multiple instruments, some I'd never seen before.

Dinner was set for 150 guests in a large community center, and there was a professional sound company setting up, as well as a professional photographer and a videographer. This was a much bigger event than we had anticipated!

We performed for about an hour to an audience of over 200 people from all the villages nearby. They were enthusiastic, clapping and singing along, and incredibly gracious with applause. When we finished, we stepped off the stage to adoring fans, hugs, and gifts from the innkeepers.

And we were exhausted.

Packed up and ready to head to our next destination the next morning, we walked with the innkeepers and their family to our car, gave and received lots of hugs, and promised to keep in touch.

A week later, we were set to play at a small café in Eygalières, Provence.

We spent the week exploring the region with Montpellier as our home base. We visited Roman ruins throughout Provence, from Arles to Nîmes, ate our way through Montpellier in the evenings, and spent a few hours relaxing on the beach. On Thursday, we drove to our next stop, St. Rémy du Provence.

It was Friday morning that we ran into our saxophone player in the market in Eygalières. He had another crazy story to share. After the previous gig, the bass player, Marco, had agreed to meet us for the second gig. He was bringing the amplifier, speaker, and microphone stand so my vocals could be amplified over the guitar, bass, and saxophone. Our friend now said that Marco might not make it for the gig the next evening . . . We had no idea what to expect, and our stress immediately jumped to danger level again.

Thank goodness, Marco arrived with gear in the late afternoon to set up and play with us for the evening. What a hero!

The gig was good, lots of people showed up, and the owner was incredibly enthusiastic about us and our music. He said that if we ever planned to come back through the area, to get in touch and play for him again.

We made our way back to Bordeaux to return the rental car, took the train back to Paris to spend two nights and one full day, and took a cab to the airport to return to Montana.

Our trip was full of adventure, fun, and yes, stress.

I'm generally someone who stays in the present moment, which means I'm not processing experiences at that time. When we returned home, there was a lot going on with our family, and I didn't have any time to decompress and reflect back on our adventure. I felt unsteady, like you feel when you've just stepped onto dry land after being at sea for a long time.

People I ran into would ask about our trip, and I'd have a chance to share a brief snippet of a story. It wasn't until I got on the phone with a virtual stranger, a connection from LinkedIn, that I began to think more deeply about the trip, and to uncover specific memories to reflect on.

I had no idea I'd be speaking with someone so insightful and kind. She asked just the right questions to help me dig into my experience at a richer and more thoughtful level. She made a couple of statements that I had to stop to think about before I could respond, and she gave me the space to do that.

She started by asking about my trip, and I gave her the quick version that only included the cities we visited.

"Tell me about the first performance. Music can open worlds, allowing real connection with people you otherwise wouldn't have a way to connect with, especially if you don't speak each other's languages."

I was suddenly transported back to that first performance on the stage of the community center, looking out at the audience. Brief, vivid memories came back to me, and I could see expressions of the other musicians on stage, the encouraging smiles on the faces of the Tahitian dancers sitting behind the stage area. I remembered stepping up onto the stage and hearing "GO, Sarah!" in French accents from behind the stage, turning to look, and the thumbs-ups and smiles of the Tahitians behind me.

Specific song performances came into my vision, like when I started to sing "Sunny," and heard a handful in the audience sing the last three words of each verse: "I love you." And getting almost everyone to sing with me on the Etta James song, "Baby Baby Every Night."

I introduced the song and asked them to say "every night" when I pointed.

> I'm gonna please you—every night
> Hug and squeeze you—every night
> I'm gonna hold your hand—every night
> And make you understand—every night
> I'm gonna love you with all my might, baby baby—every night

They were clapping, laughing, singing, and some stood up to dance.

As I shared that moment with my new friend, I felt chills on my arms. I realized I hadn't had a chance to fully remember that evening and the huge impact it had on me—and maybe on some people in the audience.

She helped me look back at specific moments, pivot points, that I could dig into more deeply when I got off the phone, and really consider the impact those moments had on the way I see myself and the world around me.

When you have someone in your life that you can trust to bring out those moments, your stories have much deeper impact. You learn more about yourself, and you have an opportunity to shrink the gap between how you see yourself and how others see you.

Recap

Processing an experience by telling the story to someone we trust who sees the best in us and our ability to persevere helps us choose learning and growth over victimhood, bitterness, and depression. Sharing that same story with someone who is a complainer, or just generally not a supportive person, will take us to the same place where they sit. We'll tell the story in their voice instead of our own, and worse, we might take on the negative self-image they're projecting on us.

Whether it's a positive story of an adventure or new relationship, or an obstacle story of challenge and even tragedy, how we share that story—and who we share it with—makes a huge difference in how we remember it, and how we internalize our messages from it.

Processing, Part 3

Panting, stopping to breathe and get my heartrate back to a reasonable pace, I looked ahead to more steep climbing up the mountain. Then I looked down at the path I had just hiked up and smiled. It was a rigorous hike, and I hadn't really planned to take such a hard trail to the summit this time.

The dog needed water, so I stopped in a shady spot just off the trail to fill his bowl and let him rehydrate. It's nice to have the dog around as an excuse to stop and catch my breath again. With his heavy fur coat, he was even less comfortable than I was on this nearly eighty-degree day before noon. But he was just as happy as I was to be outside on our mountain.

Taking one last look back, I resumed my steep climb, knowing I wasn't far from the summit.

As I listened to the randomly shuffled song that came through my headphones, I had to stop again to look up and down from the middle of the steep climb:

Glory glory, hallelujah,
The sun is shining, shining down
Glory glory, hallelujah,
I'm alive, and I'm feeling, feeling fine.

Hearing those words sung by JJ Grey in the song "The Sun is Shining Down," I started thinking about what compelled me to take this hard route to the top of the mountain. My top strengths, according to the Gallup assessment, didn't include Achiever or Competition, two of the themes I could imagine would drive someone to do what I was doing. So what was it?

It was in that moment I realized character has little to do with any assessment results.

I use my character to develop my strengths, not the other way around.

It had been a tough morning, which is why I knew I needed to hike. Getting outside always helps me clear my head and make sense of things. The email I received was cruel and unprofessional, a response to what I considered very reasonable requests for information. Words clouded my vision as I walked up the mountain, feeling attacked, defensive, angry, and self-conscious.

Had I failed in this assignment? Was it my work that triggered this unprofessional, rude response? I felt my confidence start to slip back down the mountain behind me.

Pushing myself harder, pressing my feet solidly into the slippery, rocky trail, I ascended another steep fifteen feet of the mountain.

I felt nothing but exhilaration and pride as I stepped onto the rocks at the summit. Looking down, I imagined myself when I was partway up the mountain, panting, pushing, and clearing the frustration and anxiety out of my way.

Now that I was at the top and looking back down, the path still looked crazy hard, but the feelings of inadequacy at the midpoint were no longer with me.

It was the next day, as I was telling a friend about my inspiration on the mountain, that I realized I had missed a big part of the lesson.

I told her the story with my optimistic nature showing in full force, using those words that popped into my head as I sweated and panted up the steepest part of the mountain: persistence, resilience, grit.

". . . shame, feelings of inadequacy, self-punishment . . ."

Damn. As she added those words, I realized she was right. I didn't take that hard route simply because I was demonstrating resilience and grit. I was punishing myself for what I thought I had done wrong. I was pushing away the shame I felt as I remembered the words in the email. I was proving to myself that I WAS resilient, strong, and even if I failed at one thing, I would be DAMN SURE NOT TO FAIL at this.

Our conversation shifted from why we punish ourselves to why it matters. After all, punishing myself by climbing up a mountain has to be one of the healthiest and constructive ways to do that, right?

Well, yes. But also knowing WHY I am pushing myself so hard matters. If I'm working away these feelings, these frustrations, giving those feelings a name will help me address them, specifically, rather than blowing off arbitrary steam.

When we know the why behind our actions, not only can we be more intentional about processing our feelings behind those actions; we also open our minds to learn the necessary lessons the experience can teach us.

I shared the story of my hike with my friend so I could talk through thoughts I knew could contribute to life lessons, to apply my thoughts to actual improvement in future similar situations. When we tell a story like this to a friend, we create arbitrary constraints around the experience; we create a box for the story to fit into based on prior experience. That means we look for what we want to see, set limits for understanding the context of our stories, and miss all kinds of potential for lessons and growth. But when we share the story with the right friend, they might just ask the questions we need to ask ourselves—the harder questions—and that conversation is likely to remove some of those constraints.

In the book *The Art of Possibility*, a gift I received from my friend, Jeff Ikler, the very first chapter is about exactly that: Based on past experience, we make assumptions that create a box, or constraints, for ourselves. I made assumptions based on my optimistic nature, assumptions about the reason behind the negative email I had received, assumptions about the lessons I was meant to learn from the experience. Not all of those assumptions are bad things, necessarily, but without some opportunity to question them and work through the stories I was telling myself, I may have limited my potential for personal growth.

One key element of processing this particular experience was recognizing the words I was using to describe how I saw myself that day, persistent and resilient. When I had those words in my head, I felt much better about myself. I saw the earlier experience from the perspective of being right, as opposed to being open to the possibility that I had something important to learn from it. By bringing up the other side of the equation, the likely feelings of shame and self-consciousness, and that I might be punishing myself in some way, my friend helped me see the story from a different, more vulnerable perspective. She also gave me a chance to see the difference between the words persistence and resilience.

Persistence vs. Resilience

When we share stories that demonstrate our values and character, we don't have to tell people directly that we have those values or character traits. Telling the right stories in the right way helps us model the behaviors we want to see in others, our children, and peers, without having to tell people how to behave.

There's a big difference between persistence and resilience, and the way we tell our stories can demonstrate the fine line between them. Persistence and resilience are significantly different things, and the only way to truly experience personal growth and transformation is to demonstrate both.

---

persistence

noun
the act or fact of <u>persisting</u>.
the quality of being <u>persistent</u>: *You have persistence, I'll say that for you.*
continued existence or occurrence: *the persistence of smallpox.*
the continuance of an effect after its cause is removed.

From Dictionary.com (<u>https://www.dictionary.com/browse/persistence</u>)

---

resilience

noun
the power or ability to return to the original form, position, etc., after being bent, compressed, or stretched; elasticity.
ability to recover readily from illness, depression, adversity, or the like; buoyancy.

From Dictionary.com (<u>https://www.dictionary.com/browse/resilience</u>)

By breaking down the experience with my friend, I was able to identify particular stories from my past that demonstrated those qualities, reminding myself that there is evidence in my past that not only have I been those things, I will be those things again. When I'm worried about whether I can do something, when I'm facing fear of stepping out, I look back at those stories to begin my thoughts with "All evidence points to . . ." and finish it with something that makes sense for the moment, such as ". . . my strength, resolve, creativity, and capacity to complete this project."

Your Turn

Who do you have in your life that helps you work through this kind of experience with your thoughts? Which of your friends or acquaintances can you count on to help you ask yourself the tough questions and get the most out of an experience? If you can't think of anyone right away, be intentional about building relationships with the people who can help you process your thoughts and experiences—people you can trust, be vulnerable with, and who will add positive support and encouragement. Self-reflection is a great start, but if you're not expanding that reflection by sharing it with people you trust, you're limiting your opportunities to apply that self-reflection, deepen it, and improve your communication and relationships as a result.

Helping Others Process an Experience

Think about someone in your life that consistently finds the negative in a situation. This is a person you've spent time with because you love them, because they're a family member, or simply because you've known the person for a long time and feel connected and obligated to keep them in your life. Is this a healthy relationship? When you share a story with this person, do they tell you how you failed, or that it's okay that you failed because your expectations were too high?

Are YOU that person? When someone tells you a story, do you pick it apart to find your own related, negative experience to share? Do you project your feelings of insecurity on the person in front of you?

Think about the last time you listened to someone tell a story. Did you pay attention to the details, or were you thinking about your own related story? Did you ask any questions, or did you jump right into sharing mode?

To be a good storyteller, you must be a good story listener, too.

If you have someone in your life who consistently finds the negative in life, you have a choice to make:

1. Let them know, gently, that their negativity is impacting your friendship, and/or

2. Stop spending time with them.

If you are the person with the cloud over your head all the time, you also have a choice to make:

1. Own it, and be okay with the consequences (the people you attract into your life are just like you), or

2. Adjust your stories to find the light and lessons.

I'm not suggesting that you must be positive and optimistic all the time. There are things in life that are tragic, and your feelings and responses to those things are real and relevant. But you can make the choice to find lessons and gratitude in every situation, find the beauty in a full life of experiences, and live in the moment to be the light you want to be.

CHAPTER 6

STORIES CAN BUILD AND IMPROVE OUR RELATIONSHIPS

You know now that stories can have a huge impact on your internal messages, but have you really considered how the stories you share impact the people around you and their perceptions of you?

When you hear a story from your parent or grandparent about something that happened in their youth, you can create a mental picture of them that you otherwise might completely miss.

When you're on a first date and the person in front of you starts sharing stories of their exes, what kind of impression does that leave you with?

Sharing the right story at the right time can connect you in a way nothing else can; the opposite is also true. Sharing the wrong story at the wrong time can create a major disconnect, friction, or even serious conflict.

Later in this book, you'll read some tips about storytelling that include observation of your audience. The key to using stories to build and improve relationships is choosing the right stories to share, and paying close attention to the person you're sharing them with. Their facial expressions and body language are perfect clues to how they're hearing your story!

Active Listening: The Power of Unlocking Stories in Others

We were sitting in a large circle on white folding chairs, twelve teenagers between thirteen and seventeen years old, talking about storytelling and active listening.

I had already described some of the techniques I use for active listening, like repeating words back to people to make sure I understand them, leaning forward, and making sure my body language is open and approachable, but I knew a demonstration would be more effective for the group.

Turning my chair to face the boy sitting to my right, a shy football player with his arms crossed over his chest, I started to ask him questions. I leaned forward slightly, my hands relaxed on my lap. I was fully present, and as I started the conversation, my full attention was on him; the others just faded away for me.

"I know you love sports, and that you've had some great moments playing baseball and football. What else do you do?"

"Not much. Hang out with friends, I guess."

"Do you have a dog?"

"Yes."

"What's your dog's name?"

"Henry."

"Henry! What a great name for a dog. What is his breed?"

"He's an Australian Shephard/lab mix."

"I bet he's really sweet. How do you spend time with him? Walks? Snuggles?"

"We walk together almost every day." He smiled subtly, just the edges of his lips turning upward.

"I'll bet you really love Henry and he loves you! Did you get him as a puppy, or did you adopt him?"

"We got him when he was only eight weeks old."

"Oh, how sweet. Was he super snuggly with you back then?"

"Yes."

"Do you miss his snuggly puppy days?"

He smiled sweetly this time, an obvious grin at the memory of Henry as a puppy. That's when his hands dropped into his lap, relaxed.

"I love puppies, even though they're a lot of work. Did you train Henry to do any tricks?"

"Yes, he's really smart. One time I taught him to . . ."

He went on, sharing a story of how he trained his dog to do a trick. We wrapped up the conversation, and I turned my chair to face the rest of the group.

"Anyone notice what happened there?"

Almost immediately, and almost in unison, the teens said, "Yes! He put his hands down from crossing them across his chest! He dropped his hands into his lap."

I couldn't have planned a better demonstration of the power of active listening, and that audience immediately understood that power when they saw the shift in their friend's body language. They had spent a lot of time with him but hadn't heard the story of how he trained his dog to do a trick.

If we want to truly connect with a person, we have to help them feel safe. One of the best ways to do that is to open our body language and ask questions to draw out stories. Your intention behind sharing stories and connecting with people is important. Make sure your intention is positive, nurturing, and nonjudgmental.

As you read through the next story, think about your closest relationships, friendships, and how they developed. Consider the stories you share together, years later, that make you laugh and cry as you retell and relive those adventures. When you think of those characters in the stories of your childhood and young adulthood, think about the impact they had on you—the conversations, situations, and memories created during those times spent together.

Building Relationships, Part 1

Moving from Colorado to Washington, DC, was a wonderful adventure, full of "opportunities for growth," and fun stories created. I had just graduated from college and had accepted a paid internship for the US International Trade Commission. My father offered to give my Chevette a tune-up, and to drive with me across the country, buying a one-way ticket for himself to return home.

We went straight to his sister's house when we arrived in Northern Virginia, and I went to work digging into the classified ads to find a cheap place to live near public transportation so I could park my car and not have to drive to work every day.

I ended up in a small basement apartment with very little light. It was inexpensive for that part of Northern Virginia, and the family who owned the home lived above me and were very kind. It seemed like an ideal situation for my first six months in the area, but my cat hated it. He had no windowsills to sit in and watch the world go by, and I couldn't let him out because he was unfamiliar with the area. When I got home after work, he'd attack my ankles until they were bleeding. I knew I'd have to find another place soon, but had no idea where to start, since my job paid so little and it had an automatic ending date.

Thank goodness one of my colleagues pulled a tab from one of those flyers in an office building: "Looking for roommate for two-bedroom Capitol Hill apartment." I called the number, hopeful, and Mary and I talked for nearly two hours. I moved in a few weeks later.

What did we talk about to establish that relationship without having met? We shared stories. And then we made more together.

It was late on a Friday night, probably around 10, when I told my roommate about the road trip I had taken with my sister in January that year, right before moving to Washington. She shared a story about a similar last-minute adventure with one of her college friends just a few years before. We laughed about our impulsive, adventurous lives, and suddenly looked at each other with renewed curiosity. We had been living together for three-plus months and didn't realize we had that in common.

Our eyes met, sparkling. I said, "Let's go!"

"Where?"

"Atlantic City. I was there a couple of years ago and would love to go check it out again."

"Okay!"

We packed up toothbrushes and sweatshirts, grabbed some snacks, and jumped into her car to head north. Three and a half hours later, having pulled over twice, once to get gas and use the bathroom, and once to get ourselves together because we were laughing too hard to drive, we parked the car near the boardwalk in a huge casino parking lot.

Neither of us had money to spare, so we hit the nickel slots for a few minutes so we could get a free cocktail, and then wandered around the casino.

Casinos are great places to people-watch; we sat down on a bench on the boardwalk and quietly observed everyone passing by. Every once in a while, one of us would make up an entire history for people passing us, describing in great detail what brought that person, couple, or group of friends to that point in time and place, wandering along the Atlantic City boardwalk at 2 a.m.

After practicing cartwheels on the boardwalk, making friends with bouncers and doormen at a few casinos, and getting a snack at a late-night diner, we made our way back to the car and drove home. We arrived at our apartment sometime in the early morning and went to bed.

That wasn't the last time Mary and I had an impulsive adventure; we lived together for a few years and have plenty of stories from that time together. Our stories brought out more of what we had in common, and throughout our lives as roommates we shared more stories, stories we created together. When we get together now, nearly twenty-five years later, we walk ourselves down memory lane, reliving those years. What's fascinating is that we remember the stories so differently, which is part of why we love to retell them together. Those stories keep us connected, no matter how many years we go between visits.

By sharing road trip stories early in our relationship, we identified a mutual adventurous spirit. Those stories of our lives before we met connected us.

Building and Improving Relationships, Part 2

Some stories can disconnect you from the people you care about. As you read the next story, try to remember a time when you shared the wrong story at the wrong time, alienating the person in front of you. Could you have stopped before causing damage? What was it about the story that took the conversation in the wrong direction? Was it the story itself, or was it how you were telling it?

It was the end of the summer between my senior year of high school and my freshman year of college, and my best friend and I decided to have a toga party while my parents were out of town. It got way out of hand, kids from at least four area schools showed up, and they cleaned out my parents' bar, which was full of high-end liquor. The party was broken up by the police because there were fights happening in our driveway. Our neighbors didn't complain, and my parents didn't find out, but my friend and I spent hours cleaning up and pulling cigarette butts out of the deck in the backyard.

I had a plan to replace the alcohol a little at a time, so I left the empty bottles (probably forty of them) in the bar. My parents didn't drink much, or often, so I figured they wouldn't notice. I knew they only had all of that liquor for when they had guests, for recipes, and to host parties in our home.

I was partially right; it took them a few weeks to notice, and I had only replaced the alcohol in two of the bottles.

The call from my dad came to my dorm room about the third week of school.

"Sarah. Mr. Williams came over for a visit last night, and when I went to get him some whiskey, there wasn't any in the bar. There wasn't much of anything in the bar. You told me you had some friends over while we were gone. Either you had more than fifty people over— or no one left.

"You can't snowball me on this. This is a BIG DEAL. I expect a written letter by the end of the week, telling me exactly what happened. And you owe me $300."

Hearing the cold, disappointed tone in his voice crushed me. The worst punishment I ever received from my dad were the words "I'm just so disappointed in you." He could ground me, take away privileges, whatever, but those words were way more powerful than anything else he could do.

I wrote the letter he demanded—and snowballed him with a ridiculous story about that night—but he never said another word about the incident.

In my first year in DC shortly after I graduated from college, my dad and his girlfriend came to visit. My roommate and I invited them to stay in our apartment; I gave them my room and bunked with my roommate for a few nights.

The last night of their visit, which had been really lovely, filled with good food, visits to the Smithsonian museums, and lots of time exploring together, we had dinner at a brewpub right next to Union Station near Capitol Hill.

We were laughing and swapping stories. My roommate and my father's girlfriend were asking questions about my childhood, and my father and I were sharing all kinds of fun family stories. It had been six years since the toga party/bar-clearing incident; enough time had passed, I thought, to make the story really funny.

I launched into the epic story of the huge party, the multiple high schools represented, my friend passing out after drinking nearly an entire bottle of Rompope (a Mexican liquor that tastes like vanilla pudding), the police coming to the door, the fight in the driveway, and me running around the house telling people they couldn't smoke inside.

My roommate and I were hysterical as I shared the details, my hands enthusiastically taking part in the story; we both had tears in our eyes because we were laughing so hard. I got to the part about my dad's call to the dorm room phone before I finally noticed the expression on his face and the expression of concern on his girlfriend's face as she looked at him.

But I was in too deep. I had to finish the story. Doing my best to backpedal a little, I dug myself in deeper. I could see my father getting more and more angry, but worse, I could see the sadness behind his anger. He didn't even need to say those words "I'm just so disappointed in you."

This was a story told too soon. It was probably a story I shouldn't have ever shared with my father. It still bothers me, decades later. I can see the expression on his face at that restaurant, across the booth from me. Sharing that story in that moment did some serious damage to our relationship. We eventually recovered, but our relationship, and his memory of me at that time in our lives, would never be the same.

Your Turn

What is one element of this story that resonated with you? Was it the characters? The pacing? What, if any, memories did this story trigger for you?

Sharing stories with people offers incredible opportunities to learn more about each other. By swapping stories about our road trip adventures, Mary and I discovered something about each other that encouraged us to propose completely different activities than we might have otherwise.

But sharing stories can have a downside if you're not aware of your audience and not observing their reactions as you tell your story. Are you watching your audience's response as you share? In the chapter "Storytelling Tips," I share some observation tips so you can short-circuit your story if you notice something changing in the demeanor of your audience.

What stories have you shared with people new in your life, or close friends and family, that brought your relationship to a new level, for better or for worse? Did you share those stories with intention, or did you feel pressured? How did it impact your relationship? Have you thought about that, and processed it to learn the right lessons from it?

Take a moment to look back at your story portfolio worksheet. Jot down a phrase or a sentence about a time within one of the eras you've listed when you shared the wrong story at the wrong time. Consider what you can learn from that incident; have you done that more than once?

Building and Improving Relationships, Part 3

Building relationships doesn't necessarily mean building long-term relationships. Sometimes sharing a very brief interaction and story with a stranger can have major impact that we never find out about. If we want to be known for the words we listed at the beginning of this book, the personal brand/values exercise, we have to be consistent about demonstrating those words, no matter where we are.

It's easy to make assumptions about people based on our first moments in an interaction, but if we're judging people as good or bad, smart or stupid, reliable or unreliable, based on those initial assumptions, what does that say about us?

Think about the last time someone cut you off in traffic. Did you yell, curse under your breath, or make physical gestures for them to see? Now think about your own driving. Are you always aware of the cars around you? Have you ever accidentally cut someone off in traffic? When we react to a person's behavior without considering our own faults, we aren't consistently demonstrating the values we want to see in others; we're not walking the walk.

We humans tend to judge each other harshly, regardless of our own shortcomings. Considering our own mistakes sometimes helps reduce that tendency to judge others. If you're serious about being part of the solution in terms of improving our communities, consider sharing a story of your shortcoming or error in judgment when you see someone else struggling with an accident or a poor decision.

It had to be embarrassing to one young mother when I brought her four-year-old son onto the stage between songs, in front of an audience of around 500 people from our community. One of our police officers found him wandering around the park, looking for his mom and getting scared. I figured the best way for us to connect the boy with his mom was to bring him up on stage and have him say his mother's name into the microphone. After a few stressful moments waiting for her to hear his voice, his mom came to the stage to get him, obviously filled with relief and embarrassment. She hugged him tightly and said she had been searching for him in a total panic for twenty minutes.

As she walked away with her son in her arms, I announced,

"Great! Joshua found his mom! Hasn't that happened to all of us? You only look away for a minute and your toddler can disappear. That's when your heart climbs up into your throat as you panic and start your search. It has happened to me, too; anyone else out there have this experience? It's terrifying! I'm so grateful for this community of helpers!"

It's tempting to judge, right?

It's tempting to wonder where the mom was when the toddler got lost. Wasn't she paying attention? What kind of mom does that? It's tempting to think badly of her—but that kind of thing can happen to the best parents. In reality, that mom did a great job. She gave her son the tools to recognize the situation and to seek help. When Joshua started to feel uncomfortable because he couldn't see his mom, he reached out to one of our friendliest police officers. It's a small town, which makes things a little easier. All of our officers know each other, so if there was a fake uniform at our weekly summer live music event, it would have been caught. Joshua's mom must have told that little boy many times to find a police officer if he ever got lost, and we all know it takes more than once for that kind of message to sink in. The boy wasn't too frightened—there were no tears. He knew when he hit his discomfort limit, and his good instincts led him to exactly the right person.

I shared my own story of failed parenthood, losing a toddler in a matter of seconds, to remind that mother and others that there is no place for judgment in this situation.

Have you judged too quickly? Do you have triggers that remind you not to judge? Consider a time when you shared a story of your own failure in order to connect with someone. Was it effective? Jot down a note about that in the margins here, so you can come back to it later for a reminder.

Sharing that kind of story not only builds relationships, it demonstrates a level of vulnerability that makes others feel safer to share their own concerns and worries.

"Stories constitute the single most powerful weapon in a leader's arsenal."

Dr. Howard Gardner,
Harvard University professor

CHAPTER 7

STORYTELLING FOR CAREER AND BUSINESS

E very person is "in sales." Whether the term "sales" is in your title doesn't matter. Many times each day we are selling something—usually it's ourselves, our trustworthiness, our competence, our character. That's why a consistent personal brand is so important.

Before the days of global communication networks (the internet) and social media, a company could define its brand through marketing. A company could say almost anything about its product or its leadership in an industry, and its potential customers didn't have easy access to information to question it or to find out if those things were true—unless they tried it or had direct experience with the company. That's simply not the case anymore. Not only do consumers have access to information about the company and products at their fingertips, they're likely to use easily accessible online reviews and recommendations to choose a product or service, rather than information shared by the company itself.

The same goes for an individual. Before Google and Facebook, people could generally separate their personal and professional lives. There was the saying "You never know what goes on behind closed doors." And while that statement is still true, people believe they know what goes on behind closed doors. It's easy to believe we know, because someone behind those doors is sharing all kinds of information and images. And generally, the first person to start sharing this information will be considered the trusted source.

That's why it's so important to be intentional about your behaviors and actions.

How you present yourself, no matter where you're sharing, makes a difference in how people will perceive you. Should you care what people think? Yes. Sometimes. You need to care about what certain people think of you. When it comes to personal relationships, caring about what certain people think of you can help you make decisions that are in alignment with how you want them to see you. When faced with a decision to take an action or say something unkind, I often think about what my children would think if they were to witness that action or those words.

If you have a brilliant idea or product that you want to share with the world, if you have a concept in your head that has the potential to make a positive difference in the lives of people in your community, you must care about what certain people think of you in order to share those ideas, and to develop advocates to help you get those ideas into the hands of the people you want to serve.

Caring what certain people think can make a difference in whether you will achieve your goal, and you must care about what certain people think if you know you can help them achieve their goals and improve their lives. Consider which people you want to reach and help, and then make sure you care what those particular people think about you.

When you care what certain people think of you, and you're intentional in how your actions and behaviors can support and demonstrate qualities that are in alignment with who you really are, you will see more and more opportunities to take the next step in your journey.

Opportunities don't just land in your lap. You have to position your lap to be in the right place at the right time for those opportunities to land there. That doesn't mean you have to take every opportunity you're offered; it means that if you're open to a variety of experiences and perspectives, and you can demonstrate a certain level of vulnerability through sharing your stories and your ideas, opportunities present themselves in many different ways. Most of the time we aren't as open to what's in front of us because it doesn't present itself in a way we would expect to see it, or in the way we visualized it happening.

Identifying Career Pivot Points

Whether you are an entrepreneur, business owner, leader within your organization, or have aspirations to one day be any of those, knowing your career pivot points and how to talk about them will greatly improve your potential for positive impact on the people around you.

What these pivot points ARE NOT:

- They are not broad strokes to describe discomfort, success, or failure.
- They do not refer to a long period of time (more than a few days or months).
- They are not epic stories of near-death, celebrity sighting, or overnight success.
- They are not JUST related to your business.

What these pivot points ARE:

- They are SPECIFIC moments in time: a significant conversation, event, adventure, project.

- They are meaningful in terms of how they shifted the way you see the world and your role in it, good and bad.

- They involve specific people and places that you can describe in detail in terms of what they looked like, where you were, what feelings you had before, during, and after.

- They are moments that you probably didn't know were pivotal at the time they were happening, but when you look back, you see how that moment changed your trajectory, mindset, and substantially impacted your relationship with yourself and others.

People want to hear about specific times in your career that you took a risk, struggled, succeeded against the odds, were mentored by someone or mentored someone, and when you knew you were in exactly the right place, doing exactly what you knew you were meant to do. They want to know the details so they can relate to the emotions you've experienced; they need to sense your vulnerability in order to connect with you and truly see their own future through those lenses.

You may not be aware of the stories you have to share that fit those categories, thus limiting your ability to connect with people one-to-one, through interviews, public speaking, and even participating in meetings, conferences, and mentoring opportunities. You may also be missing key opportunities to uncover your own internal messages that are hindering your progress and success in relationships.

When you begin the next series of exercises, remember that these stories must be specific, describing an incident, conversation, or event that you may think wouldn't be exciting or interesting to others. As your memories begin to come back to you, let the images flood your brain, and try to solidify them by jotting down detailed notes about what you're remembering: eye color, facial expressions, colors of walls, clothing, observations of physical dynamics such as where you were sitting, how the person moved or walked. Let the images come back to you in as much detail as possible.

I suggest you take just a few minutes to jot down those details, and then let them simmer in your head for a few hours or a day, giving your brain time to conjure more vivid details.

Remember that as you are pulling up these memories, the way you share them has the potential to change the perception your listeners have of you. What parts of the story will demonstrate those qualities you wrote down in the personal brand exercise earlier in the book? Consider the aspects of your story that may come across as arrogant or negative; think about how to shift the focus of the story slightly away from you by describing the other people involved, those people who influenced you in a positive way. If every story is about you, and no other characters are introduced, you will lose your audience. Think about the TV shows, movies, and plays that you love. Is there just one character? Make sure your stories include other people, because no one changes, transforms, or experiences life completely alone.

I always begin with a relevant story in every keynote, workshop, and interview. It's critical to collect a portfolio of these stories to share, that demonstrate specific experiences in your career that you know had a huge impact on you, your career, and the people in your life.

Identifying Career Pivot Points: A Story

I hadn't planned to have children. When I was in my early teens, I had some pretty awful babysitting experiences. And in my late teens and early twenties, I took a lot of physical risks, like hitchhiking through New Zealand alone, and I realized I could barely take care of myself—there was no way I could be responsible for taking care of others.

Very early in our dating life, I made sure my husband knew I had no interest in having children. And though I knew he had wanted children, he wanted me more. A few months after we were married, I saw him helping his six-year-old niece fish off the pier at his father's place in southeastern Virginia, and my mind almost instantly changed. It seemed like such a waste for him not to have children. Watching him speak with her so tenderly, gently guiding her hands to help her bait the hook, and cast her line, I realized at least one child was in our future.

In the last part of my pregnancy, I hired a nanny and had everything set up so I could go back to work shortly after the baby was born. And four weeks after his birth, I went back to work three days each week, leaving him with the nanny from 7:30 a.m. until at least 6:30 p.m. Tuesday, Wednesday, and Thursday; my commute from Washington, DC, to Baltimore was nearly an hour.

After three weeks of this schedule, I came home completely exhausted, as usual, unloaded the breast milk I had pumped during the day into the freezer, and took the baby from the nanny to nurse him. She left, and I sat down on the couch with the phone, dialing my mother's number as the baby latched on hungrily.

I was looking down at his beautiful face, noticing his long, dark eyelashes, when my mother picked up and said hello.

I suddenly couldn't speak. I was sobbing so hard I could barely breathe. The tears came from out of nowhere, and I couldn't stop weeping. My mother started to panic. As a baby nurse, she knew far too much about what could happen early in an infant's life, what postpartum depression looked like, etc. I could hear the intensity in her voice when she said, "Sarah. Please tell me what's wrong. You're really worrying me. Is the baby okay? Tell me you and the baby are okay. Please."

Holding my breath for a moment, I was finally able to speak.

"It's just that . . . now I know how much you love me."

She was quiet. We sat for a few minutes just listening to each other cry.

We talked a little about our days, caught up for a few minutes, and when my husband walked into the apartment, we each said "I love you" and hung up.

During dinner that night, my husband and I talked about what changes we would have to consider if one of us were to stay home more with our son, and decided to start looking for jobs outside of DC, where we could live more easily on less income. The idea of moving to Montana was born that night, and about five weeks later we were packing up a Ryder truck with a car trailer and driving across the country.

Up until that moment, I hadn't considered what an alternate life would look like; I had been so single-minded about my career that it hadn't even occurred to me to stay home.

What's fascinating about this story, which probably lasted less than fifteen minutes, is that it wasn't until years later, as we were discussing my going back to work, that I realized what a pivotal moment that phone call was.

It was the moment a seed was planted that would completely change my world, and my vision of my future. That phone call woke me to an internal shift of priorities that would forever alter who I thought I was, and to what lengths I would go to demonstrate that love, the intensity of those tears, to our child.

Exercise 1

Think about a time, early in your career, that you took on a project or job you felt unprepared for and unqualified to do. Now jot down a few details about it.

Who were the people involved?

Was there one particular person who was especially encouraging/supportive, or discouraging/difficult?

Why did you choose to take that risk?

What were the steps you took at the very beginning of the project, and what were the missteps early on?

What miscommunications happened along the way?

Write the conclusion to the story:

Did you succeed?

Did you fail?

What happened immediately afterward?

What lessons did you learn?

Write the details of two specific conversations with people you remember clearly, conversations that were either very difficult or very satisfying.

Exercise 2

Again, thinking about a time early in your career, try to remember a specific incident that, when you look back now, you realize had a major impact on your current work, beliefs, attitude, and motivation. What incident, event, situation, or influence/person motivated you to be where you are right now, doing what you do?

What exactly was the incident or situation?

Who was there with you?

What relationship did you have with the other people involved?

Did anyone do or say anything that still sticks with you years later? Something insulting, inspiring, or insightful?

What did you learn about yourself from the situation? Did it change how you saw yourself at that time?

Exercise 3

Consider your work over the past five years, and think about a specific incident or event that made you realize you were exactly where you needed to be, where you were supposed to be. Think about a client or colleague that you were able to make a difference with, simply because you were able to connect with them or think about a project differently from how others were thinking about it.

What was the situation, and why did you walk away feeling so satisfied and successful in that moment?

Who were the people involved? Jot down details about the people, add any context for them that you can—where they grew up, where they were in their career, what kinds of influences they had, hobbies, family life, etc. Give the characters in your story as much detail as you can, so they feel real and vivid to you and to your potential listeners.

Don't stop with these three exercises. Now that you're digging into those memories, keep the momentum going and think about as many of those career pivot points as you can. Write yourself notes in the worksheet section of the book, under career pivot points, to remind yourself of the stories you want to come back to, develop and give more context to, and potentially use in future communications.

Revealing Patterns

As you build your story portfolio, you begin to dig into specific incidents during pivot points or eras in your life, and you can see the patterns that start to emerge. In your professional life, identifying patterns can help you address certain challenges in order to move forward. The best way to identify patterns at work is to consider the stories you share about work. Think about how you would describe each of your supervisors or bosses from your past. Think about the stories you share about your career: Are they mostly positive? Do you tend to get into a complaint-filled rant about how you have been treated at multiple jobs, with multiple coworkers and bosses?

Ask someone who has known you through multiple jobs what stories you've shared with them over the years. The ones they remember are the ones you may want to add to your story portfolio.

If you are a victim in the majority of your work stories, the one thing that has been consistent in each of those positions was you.

Identify the patterns, and then you can be intentional about whether you want to—or need to—change them.

Emerging Patterns at Work, Part 1

After two years in the position, I found myself standing in the bathroom with a tear-stained face . . . again. What was wrong with me? Why couldn't I make this work? I'm not a particularly emotional person, and yet here I was with swollen eyes and a runny nose. . . again. Why was I letting my boss get to me like this?

This wasn't the first time I found myself struggling with an abusive boss in a bad environment. Just two positions before this one, I had another abusive boss. As I stood looking in the mirror, my reflection said it all: You've been in this position before that, too.

I started to look back at all of my jobs, all the way back to being a food server at an IHOP in college. There were some exceptions; I did experience jobs where I was valued, where I thrived and became the professional person I am today. Looking back, though, there were far too many similar situations in my past. This was a pattern.

It took some deep self-reflection to come to this conclusion, the most humbling and difficult moment in my career.

I had some complicity here.

What an awful realization. Who wants that kind of answer to a question? No one I know wants to admit they did something wrong or that they played a part in what was wrong with a relationship or job.

I'm not for a second suggesting that bullying and abuse is the fault of the victim. I'm not for a second suggesting that it is ever okay to treat people badly or that a victim has somehow earned abuse. There are circumstances and patterns, though, that when we see them in our lives can awaken us to our role in our own successes and challenges, if we take responsibility as adults and choose to make changes.

The pattern emerged, beginning in a high school job at a T-shirt shop inside the mall, when my coworker, the owner's daughter, gave me a hard time about flirting with customers, and shortly after that incident, her mother fired me. Then there was the camp counselor position between high school and my freshman year of college, when the camp director undermined me with my campers, and didn't correct the rumor among other staff about how I got my job.

In my first job as a cocktail waitress, when the manager treated me differently from how she treated the rest of the waitresses after she told me I took far too much time visiting with my customers. And then again in a restaurant where I served during my internship in Washington, DC, to make ends meet; the manager fired me shortly after a sous chef asked me out on a date.

As I stood looking in the mirror, I could see the faces of the people I felt had abused me in some way in the workplace. The pattern of my behavior in those environments started to take shape in my mind, but I didn't have time to fully consider that; I had to go back to my desk and do my job—well.

Looking in the mirror again, gently dabbing a damp paper towel around my tear-stained eyes, I walked back to my desk. Curiosity replaced sadness and anxiety as I explored those memories and became more of an observer than an active player in the actions and behaviors of my boss.

It took a few weeks to fully process what I was seeing, because those jobs were all so different from each other, and because the people I worked with in each of those jobs had completely different backgrounds. The experiences were different, but the feelings I had were the same.

What I noticed was that I have a habit of taking control of situations, even when I'm not "supposed" to be managing or leading. I give the impression of authority when I don't have authority, and I have generally cared more about the people I was working with, my customers and peers, than I cared about the specific job I was doing.

When I looked at the pattern, I could see that I wasn't necessarily doing anything wrong; it was how I was presenting myself, often without considering the needs, feelings, and insecurities of the people I worked for. Either they thought I wanted their job, thought I was bossy or a know-it-all, or they thought I was too nice. There may have been other reasons for the pattern, and for me to address my pattern, I had to lean into those reasons to find my own behaviors that had contributed to their discomfort around me. Again, I had to replace my victim mentality with curiosity and intention to grow and change my patterns.

At that point, it wasn't about whether I cared what those people from the past thought of me, or whether they were right or wrong; it was about my survival in the working world, and how I was contributing to my own obstacles in that world.

I'd love to be able to report that it was like a light going on in my brain and that I was able to turn around the damaged relationship with my boss at that job after this reflection, but I can't. I wasn't the only one in that relationship, and it takes both parties, and intention and willingness to acknowledge our roles in the situation.

Things did gradually change and improve for me in that job, though, as I realized some of my behaviors that were contributing to her discomfort around me and made efforts to adjust them. Even more important was my awareness of this pattern when I started a new job a few months later and was able to apply those lessons.

Your Turn

Take a few minutes to think about a time that you realized you might have played a role in a difficult situation with someone, but didn't necessarily take responsibility for it. It may be that you unintentionally but subconsciously knew you were antagonizing someone, possibly with the thought that you were "just doing your job," or "just being honest," or "just being your authentic self," but could have presented information differently if you had considered for a bit longer how that person was going to react to something you did or said.

This is one of those unpleasant sides to self-reflection, and it's absolutely necessary for uncovering patterns that are contributing to dissatisfaction in relationships at work and at home.

The situations you think about here may come back to an abusive situation, where nothing you could have said or done differently would have changed the outcome. In that case, perhaps your role, the lesson you are meant to find in uncovering this story or these stories, is that you must begin to stand up for yourself, and pay attention to the red flags you might be ignoring about the people you are bringing into your life. It's just as important, if not more important, to know when you couldn't have changed a situation, and stop blaming yourself for it, while understanding how you got into it in the first place.

Again, make notes in the margins of the book to mark parts of the stories that are bringing up memories for you, so you can go back to them and add those stories to your story portfolio later, as the details start to emerge from your memory.

Emerging Patterns at Work, Part 2

I was preparing myself for my evaluation because I knew it would not be pleasant. That morning I noticed on the calendar appointment that my supervisor had invited her supervisor to sit in with us; she didn't let me know ahead of time. When I asked her about it she was noncommittal: "I'm allowed to invite someone to join us."

The year had been tumultuous, to say the least. It was a position completely out of my comfort zone, a complete 180 degrees from the human side of grant work to the finance and compliance side of a multimillion-dollar grant. I knew early in the project that my supervisor was not my biggest fan when she said, "I don't know why they hired you. You have none of the qualifications for this job."

The work was a stretch for me, but I was confident that with support I would be successful. I asked for guidance when I wasn't sure what I was supposed to be doing, and my work to that point had been well received. The quarterly reports I submitted to our funders were getting rave reviews; at one point, the funders asked to use our quarterly reports as an example for other grantees. My relationship with my boss was substantially more challenging than the work.

Was I a perfect employee? Nope. I was learning new skills—personal and professional—every single day. It wasn't easy.

As I was mentally preparing for the evaluation, I called my friend to talk me off the ledge. I was near tears with worry, my hands were shaking, my palms were sweaty, and I could feel my heart pounding. I had ten minutes. My very wise friend's advice was this:

When you're in the room, imagine there's a video being recorded. Imagine you will view that video in ten years. Imagine how you want to see yourself when you view that video in the future. Will you be pleased with yourself? Or embarrassed? Will you wish you handled things differently?

I sat in that small, closed-door room and imagined a camera catching the entire discussion. Every time I felt the urge to be defensive or to respond in anger, I would remember my friend's awesome advice. I imagined seeing myself in ten years with a Mona Lisa smile on my face. My supervisor seemed to try very hard to get me to react in anger. I could see her frustration at not being able to point and say "See? This is why I can't work with her!" Her supervisor sat quietly, barely looking up from her notepad, obviously uncomfortable with the tone my supervisor was taking in this evaluation, the direction of the comments toward personal attack and away from constructive feedback.

The imaginary video camera caught me with my Mona Lisa smile, leaning forward just slightly to indicate good listening posture, and then slowly leaning back slightly to demonstrate my comfort in my skin. It caught me responding to her concerns with answers like

"Hmm. I can see why there was miscommunication about that."

And "It must have been frustrating for you. I didn't intend to be insulting. Here's how I thought that conversation went."

The meeting was over, and I smiled as I opened the door for my supervisor and her supervisor. Her supervisor and I had agreed on a course of action to correct some of my misunderstandings about the internal financial system, and to schedule a meeting so I could explain how I had created our quarterly reports.

It was time to take a walk, breathe, and assess. I had a genuine smile on my face for the first time in days. I saw my supervisor walking the other direction, a grimace on her face, clearly aggravated. It made me a little sad. My relief should not have been reason for her frustration. But that wasn't mine; I didn't own it.

I imagined watching that video sometime in the future; I was satisfied with how I handled the situation, and I was confident that when I watched it, I'd see myself in the meeting demonstrating grace, compassion, and dignity.

Your Turn

Have you been in a meeting or conversation that you walked away from feeling like you could have handled it better? Think about a time you walked into a meeting you knew was not going to be pleasant, where you felt unprepared in any way, or felt like you or your ideas were going to be attacked. How did you handle it? Could you have used this strategy to slow down the meeting and your emotions in order to choose how to react, rather than react immediately and maybe regret saying something?

Think about your facial expressions and body language in the meeting or conversation: Could you have given an unintended or damaging impression of anger, defensiveness, ambivalence, or resignation?

Emerging Patterns at Work, Part 3

My mouse hovered over the send button.

The email message was pointed—direct—and I felt strongly that these words needed to be shared with my boss and a director of the agency. But I hesitated as my mouse hovered.

I had felt lethargic throughout the weekend. From the time I left the office on Friday evening until Tuesday morning, I couldn't shake this lack of motivation. A few minutes after I sat down at my desk on that Tuesday morning, I looked up at my calendar, and the lightbulb in my head went on. Monday had been my two-year anniversary at that job.

When I left my previous position, I made a "deal-breaker" list. It was basically my top priorities for my next job. A micromanaging, cruel boss was at the top of my list of deal breakers. Next was my workspace. An internal cubical, small and without windows, was also a deal breaker. There were a few others, but those were the big ones.

As I walked into the building for my third interview, and was shown to what would be my third-floor office with huge windows and a fantastic view, I knew this would be mine. And here I was, exactly two years later, feeling lethargic and sad despite this phenomenal view from my desk.

I shifted the mouse pointer away from the send button and reread the message.

A memory from my previous position floated to the front of my brain.

My mouse pointer had hovered dangerously over the send button two years prior, at my previous job. I absolutely knew this message was likely to create some drama with my boss. I rationalized hitting the send button: "It's a reasonable thing to forward. I'm not doing anything wrong."

I totally underestimated the drama, and seconds after I hit the button, my boss was next to my desk, her voice rising in tone and volume. I blushed, angry at the overreaction and embarrassed at the attention she was drawing to our cubicle, trying to explain why I sent the email. Nothing I said made a difference, and she stomped away from me, furious.

A few minutes later, as I was walking around the building to get some fresh air and perspective, it dawned on me. I totally earned that embarrassment. I poked the bear. I knew I was going to poke the bear. I knew I was antagonizing her when I hit the send button on that message. No matter how rational and reasonable the content of that message, I knew I was stirring up trouble and I did it anyway.

Why?

At that point in my job, I was in maintenance mode. I had set up systems to manage reporting and compliance, and most of my days were spent reviewing spreadsheets and building reports based on the data I was collecting. It was relatively quiet in our team that week, and I was probably bored, so I sabotaged myself.

Fast-forward two years later as my mouse pointer hovered over the send button, my memory of the other experience vivid and ready to be applied. I stopped myself. I reflected. I was bored, and I was about to sabotage myself . . . again.

I realized that if I was bored, it was up to me to find a more constructive way to address it. In that job, I had a lot of autonomy and freedom to work on projects, so I took some time to think about what I wanted to learn more about, what projects would truly benefit the organization and our community, and those I could persuade my boss and other leaders in the organization to support and implement. Making a list and starting to carefully word my next proposal, I saved that email message for another time, and as a reminder to avoid sabotaging myself again.

Emerging Patterns at Work, Part 4

Our relationship got off on the wrong foot on my very first day of work. As my colleague walked me through the building to introduce me around at my new job, I already knew at least half of the people she tried to introduce me to, and they gave me a warm welcome with hugs and smiles. Her expression was one of disappointment and frustration. I'm not sure why this particular colleague was tasked to walk me around on my first day, but I'm guessing it was because we were expected to work together regularly. Our jobs intersected a lot, though we were in two different departments.

She had introduced me as the "new Linda," my predecessor in that job, and I was quick to let people know that the job description had changed, and I described some of what I was hoping to bring to that role. It seems petty now, but I don't like to be referred to as "the new" anyone, as if any one person is replaceable or an individual can be labeled with the name of a predecessor.

Apparently, Linda was her very good friend, and my guide through the building found my comments insulting. I didn't know until at least a year later, long after our hostile relationship had settled in.

Despite the fact that our offices would have been much better served if we worked together and got along, I managed to avoid interaction with her most of the time. When I did have to ask her a question or follow up about anything after a meeting, I was sugary sweet and generally walked on eggshells to avoid a confrontation with her. It just wasn't going to benefit my work—or our customers— to antagonize her.

What I didn't know was that it didn't matter what I did or how nice I was to her. She hated me, and it had nothing to do with me. My colleague and her friend, my predecessor, had tried to manipulate the situation before I started; because she wanted my job. But the CEO and human resources director changed the job description and added certain skills and education requirements, and she no longer qualified for the position. Leadership tried to placate the woman by putting her on the hiring committee. That made things worse because they hired me, not the person she rated highest on the interview worksheets.

It had been two and a half years, and that relationship never got beyond prickly.

I had to ask her a question, so I walked into her office, smiling sweetly.

My approach was direct:

"I don't have a copy of the document that was attached to last week's meeting agenda. Would you please email that to me?"

"Fine."

"And I was hoping to talk to you about an idea I had, a process to make things a little simpler and more accessible for our staff and customers."

She went from icy cold to furious and loud: "Oh, I know ALL about your idea, SARAH. And you should have come to me FIRST."

I saw the blush creeping up her neck to her face as she told me how angry she was with me. She sat at her desk, the tension visible in her body, while I stood in front of her desk, feeling my own face flush with embarrassment and frustration.

I had worked hard to avoid upsetting her, taking a lot of my lessons from my previous position and thoughtfully applying them. Now I knew that no matter how hard I tried, some situations required a different response. In this case, I simply had to stand up for myself and call her on her bad behavior.

"You should have come to ME first, not your boss. He doesn't know anything. You went around me and I'm really MAD at YOU."

"Carla, if I have a choice between talking to you and talking to him, I'll always go to him first because you're not nice to me. You're dismissive, rude, and you talk behind my back."

I had startled her. She was not prepared for me to fire back. Her face flushed more as she responded.

"We've had a communication problem between our offices since you started. I've been here for over twenty years, and I'm NOT going to let you ruin my last two years before I retire."

It took everything in me to respond with courtesy and calm, and all the lessons I had learned in the previous position were suddenly in front of me, ready for application. I imagined being recorded again, and wanting to see myself in a particular light when I watched it in a few years.

"My office is forty feet down the hall from yours. You haven't set foot in my office in two years. If there is a communication problem, it might just be coming from here. I've worked hard to avoid antagonizing you for more than two years; I've gone out of my way to be kind, despite your behavior toward me. If you don't want to ruin your last two years here, that has nothing to do with me."

Again, she flushed a deeper red, realizing I wasn't going to back down, so she turned it into a personal insult.

"We will NEVER be friends."

I smiled my Mona Lisa smile and said, "I'm okay with that."

We finished our heated conversation with an agreement to behave professionally, that she would "try not to dismiss me."

As I stepped back into my office and sat at my desk, I knew something in me and in our relationship had profoundly changed. I imagined a video playing that episode back to me a year into the future and knew I could be proud of my response. I didn't insult her; I pointed out her unprofessional behavior. I didn't get angry. And most important, I didn't take her abuse personally.

That story of taking abuse, that internal message of being a victim, had shifted. The pattern was broken. Of course, I must continue to practice standing up for myself in a way that feels authentic, not aggressive. The pattern was broken in that moment, but could reappear if I'm not paying attention to my environment and the people in it. By retelling the story periodically, I am reminded of the pattern I broke, and am able to call on the feelings that emerged following that interaction.

Your Turn

I learned a lot of lessons in those two-plus years. I continue to face similar challenges; now I'm more aware of my actions that might be contributing to the problems.

Which patterns are you noticing in your most difficult situations and relationships?

When you identify those patterns, and can see your role in them, you can break or adjust them. Until you identify your patterns, you will continue to face similar situations. If your most common experiences at work or with romantic partners are similar, the common piece of the puzzle is you. This is where you can get into trouble with the word *authenticity*.

If you say "I don't care what people think of me" often, and are dissatisfied with your work life and other relationships, you must make a choice. Either understand the consequences of your behavior, those "authentic" qualities you demonstrate that are contributing to your dissatisfaction, and be okay with those consequences, or choose to make changes in the stories you tell yourself and others to address those qualities.

Rewrite those stories into your future. Make the necessary changes to take responsibility for your patterns.

Interviews

"Tell me about yourself" has to be one of the worst interview questions—or general questions—ever asked. If you really want to know about a person, ask them something more specific, like where they grew up, what book they're currently reading, or their favorite movie.

Whether it's a job interview, a podcast, or multimedia interview, or simply a conversation with a potential client, unfortunately almost every interview includes some version of that request. That's why it's so important to be prepared with a story that demonstrates the qualities you want the interviewer to see and understand in you.

Job Interviews

Begin by reviewing the job description, and try to predict some of the questions you are likely to be asked. Dig into the company's website for clues about the culture. Make sure you've seen their mission statement if they have one!

Prepare to share stories from your experience that fit with what appears to be a common theme or image for the organization. If you have a contact there, ask what questions might be asked during the interview.

Search online for interview questions related to the position title or description; you'll find a handful of common questions.

Next, look at your résumé or application. Do you have a brief story about an accomplishment from each of your positions? Think about the most relevant experience you have for the position you're interviewing for, and prepare two stories you can share that truly demonstrate an accomplishment in that position.

Your selected stories must . . .

- Apply to the question! Make sure you're answering the question that was asked.

- Provide details about the context of the situation and the people involved.

- Provide a specific action you took to solve a problem.

- Describe the other people in the situation who were affected and/or involved in the solution (teamwork, credit where credit is due).

- Provide a clear indication of how the story ends (the accomplishment, and its effect on you, the customer, and the organization).

One of my favorite LinkedIn publishers, Lou Adler, offers his "most important interview question of all time":

Think about your most significant accomplishment. Now, tell me all about it.

Even if that specific question isn't asked, be prepared to answer questions with detailed, appropriate and applicable stories. If you do that well, you will leave the interview more satisfied, even if you don't get the job.

Job Interviews, Part 1

It felt right, sitting at the table being interviewed by a group that was clearly inspired and committed to their jobs with the community college. I knew two of the six people in that interview, thanks to my recent position with the university system.

I had predicted most of the questions so far, and was prepared with specific examples of project coordination and relationship building. It was when they asked me about how I would handle a critical situation at work that I had an opportunity to add humor and a major accomplishment to the mix.

"Tell us how you would handle a critical situation at work."

"Critical situation? A heart attack is a critical situation. I work for the university system, and my work is important, but critical? I'm not a doctor!"

They all laughed as I dove into a story.

As part of my responsibility to improve transfers among students in our system, I was working with faculty all over the state to find what could be considered equivalent courses among their offerings, and to give those courses the same course names and identifying numbers for the catalogs. When meeting with faculty from a specific subject area, like math or biology, I kept track of our discussion using spreadsheets.

I recently prepared to facilitate those discussions with biology faculty from across the state by creating a spreadsheet listing every biology course offered at every school. There were over 700 courses listed. Each line included the name of the school, the current course number, the current course name, and a brief description of it. The spreadsheet was then sorted by course number, so we would have the 100-level courses together, etc. To the right of each line was space for a placeholder number and name that would be the same for each course the group decided might be equivalent.

The spreadsheets were critical to the success of the transfer initiative, because each subject-area spreadsheet, when completed, was used to create a map for students, advisors, and faculty to address the needs of students transferring between state schools. The spreadsheets were incredibly detailed, and thousands of people were depending on them to be accurate.

We spent more than eight hours together, going through each course one at a time to talk about the outcomes expected when a student passed it. Every time we found a course we thought was equivalent to another, I would enter the placeholder name and number to the right of each course.

I know about spreadsheets; that was the majority of my work in this position, and I had become a master at navigating them. Any time I was going to sort one, I selected every column of the table to make sure it sorted the entire table, not just the selected rows and columns.

When we returned to the office after the biology faculty meeting, it was time for me to organize that list of over 700 biology classes, pick out the ones we tentatively agreed were equivalent, and follow up by collecting syllabi and a list of expected outcomes for each.

I must have worked on that spreadsheet for close to ten hours that week, painstakingly (and lovingly) color-coding and adding outcomes.

It was a level of detail I was used to, but my eyes were exhausted!

I sent it off to the team to review, and moved on to the next subject area: math.

It was about two weeks later that I opened it up again, after a few other people had looked at it and saved any edits they made. We had a plan for version control, so I was confident I was working on the most recent version.

But as I started to look through the list, something caught my attention; I have a very visual memory, and a couple of the courses listed for one university didn't look quite right.

I opened the very first version I created, with the entire list, and a lump caught in my throat. Somewhere in our versions, the list got mixed up. Someone had resorted the list without including the column with the school name.

I had to alert the team immediately. We had all put hours of work into the list, and with that level of detail, I was concerned that I wouldn't be able to catch everything. Our team meeting was not pleasant, and we had no idea which of us had messed up. It was seriously stressful, and all agreed with my strategy to find the most recent spreadsheet that was sorted correctly.

I carefully went through each version to compare it with the original, starting with the most recent one, and worked my way backward. It took a long time to find the most recent version with the correct courses associated with the correct school. Then I started the painful process of recreating the changes the team had made.

It didn't feel like there was a choice in this scenario; I simply had to hunker down and fix it. The most difficult parts of the situation were talking to the team and then following up with the faculty who had spent so much time working through this. I had to tell them about the mistake and assure them that we could fix it without them having to spend a lot more time on the project. Those conversations were awkward and stressful. But every time I finished one, I felt a sense of relief and pride in the team we created.

It took hours of deep gazing into spreadsheets, but I did it—I recovered all the work our team and the faculty had put into it.

Everyone on the interview team smiled at me as I finished telling the story. It had just enough detail for them to understand the context of the problem, and a few of them were familiar enough with the project that they recognized the significance of the "critical" problem I worked with the team to solve.

I didn't get the job, though I was one of two final candidates after that interview. When I asked my friend on the selection committee for feedback, to let me know what I did or said that might have contributed to my not getting the job, she said,

"Sarah, you did great. Everyone had a hard time with the selection, partly because of the stories you shared that clearly revealed your attention to detail, your concern for your team and those you serve, your sense of humor, and your willingness to put in the hard work. The other candidate had a large local network that would make it faster and easier for this project to move quickly, and that's what they considered when it came down to the decision."

Your Turn

What did my interviewers hear in this story? What kinds of values did I demonstrate with it? Consider the stories of your work experiences, and add three to your story portfolio.

Job Interviews, Part 2

The question in the interview for a customer experience position was "Can you tell us how you handled a difficult customer?"

Here's the story I shared for the answer:

I was the only person at the circulation desk at our public library. She walked in five minutes before closing time. Her determined steps toward the counter made me want to walk to the back and pretend no one was at the desk. It must have been humid outside because her hair was frizzed out, and even her eyebrows looked angry. Or maybe she was creating an electric current in her pace.

This was a patron I had seen before and knew could be difficult, so when she walked up to the circulation desk, I accidentally took a step back.

"I'm NOT paying for this lost book because I DID NOT LOSE IT. I just paid for one of those stupid [interlibrary loan] envelopes and I'm NOT paying for another one. I know I'll probably lose my library privileges over this but I'm NOT paying because I KNOW I TURNED IN THE BOOK.

"You people are incompetent, losing things and not marking them as turned in. The next time I turn in an interlibrary loan book, I'm going to make the person sign a paper saying I turned it in!"

With this, she tossed the letter she had received about the overdue book across the circulation desk.

I felt myself blush, my cheeks flushing with discomfort. It was tempting to treat her with the same disrespect she was treating me. I took a breath, realizing that if I got angry, the situation would get worse, and I would be even later in locking up the library and going home.

"I understand that you're frustrated; I'm sure we can figure this out. I'll put a note on your account that says you're sure you turned in the book. I'll talk to my supervisor about this tomorrow, and we'll be in touch with a solution. Maybe with your suggestions, we can come up with an additional check-in process like you suggest.

"In the meantime, would you please check under the seats of your car again? Sometimes these slippery envelopes slide right under the seat when you stop." She glared at me.

She followed me to the copier so I could copy her letter, and she watched as I wrote a note to my supervisor. She left the library twenty minutes after closing time.

My family was waiting for me to eat dinner, and though they were understanding about my coming home late, I was frustrated and prickly. When we sat down to eat, I told them the story of the last-minute patron I had to deal with, from the description of her as she walked into the library, to the way she slammed the door of her car when she left.

They were able to find humor in it, providing the distraction and perspective I needed to calm down. We talked about the book I would write about customer service, focusing on the fact that if you want good customer service, you should start by being a good customer! The title? *How to Get What You Want and Have People Love You for It.*

The next morning during my shift, I watched her walk into the library, and she saw me at the desk. Her apology sounded forced, her voice scratchy and low.

"I'm here to eat crow."

She addressed me three feet away from the circulation desk, then tossed the book inside the envelope on top of the desk—it slid to within a few inches of me and nearly fell to the floor before I stepped over to catch it.

"The book! That's great! Where did you find it?" I smiled, genuinely relieved that she found it. She didn't seem relieved. If anything, she seemed almost disappointed, and definitely defensive.

"Under the seat of my car." That's when I asked whether she wanted me to sign something to prove that she turned it in. She said no.

When the person interviewing me asked how I could be so calm and patient, I said that every customer has a life prior to an interaction with me, good and bad.

"I'm not always kind. I'm human, and there are days when I don't present the best version of myself. But when I can take a step back and remind myself that the person in front of me is also human, flawed, and probably in some discomfort or pain, I find a lot more internal strength to be kind."

Your Turn

Again, consider a specific incident in your recent work life that demonstrates the values you know an interviewer is looking for. Think about a customer, internal or external, that you were able to help, either to find a resolution to their problem, or just by listening so they could vent and calm down. Add at least one story to your portfolio under a heading labeled *Interview Stories*.

"Tell us about how you handled a difficult customer." Almost every service-type position interview includes this question or something along these lines. The answer to this question, or one about dealing with difficult employees, reveals a lot about the candidate. Can you share a story that truly demonstrates who you are and how you relate to others?

Other Interviews

I've been interviewing people for my podcast for a few years now, and I can count on one hand the professionals who were able to share a relevant, personal story without hesitation or coaching from me. It's likely a combination of their brain freezing, that moment when someone asks you a question and your mind just goes blank, and the self-consciousness that comes with sharing a personal story.

Many people I've worked with over the years tell me they just don't have any stories to share, or that they're not good storytellers.

Everyone has stories. If you are ambitious at all, if you intend to inspire others and help them grow, you need to learn to tell relevant, personal stories really well.

In preparation for any interview, ask the interviewer for context, themes, major topics they want to discuss. Have a few of your own topics ready to suggest, based on your expertise and the stories you know will demonstrate the qualities you need to share.

Other Interviews

I was being interviewed by Jordan Gross about a "cloud nine" moment. He asked me to describe a recent cloud nine moment, a situation or event that brought me great satisfaction and happiness.

"Just yesterday, actually. I was speaking with a coaching client about an internal message that continued to plague her, a message of inadequacy. She told me that early on in her career, a boss was constantly criticizing her, nitpicking everything she did. I asked her to share a specific time her boss did this, and she was able to remember details about a project she had completed, why she felt so good about the successful completion of it, and what her boss said had gone wrong. As we drilled down into the boss's mind space at that time, she started to understand why he had been so picky. She realized his concerns about the details had nothing to do with her, or the quality of her work. It was about his lack of self-confidence in presenting it to the client. In the end, the client loved her work, but his criticism of it had stuck with her for years.

"After she understood the context of his comments, talking through the story with that in mind, I could see the internal message shifting. I could see the look in her eyes as she recalled other false evidence of her inadequacy in the context of that experience. Her entire demeanor changed, and I knew that, over time, her confidence would improve."

When I finished the story, Jordan was grinning from ear to ear. I didn't have a one-line answer to my cloud nine moment question; I told a story to demonstrate why it was meaningful. Think about the difference for a moment, and think about how a listener would be able to relate to the story so much more deeply than if I had shared a one-sentence cloud nine moment!

Your Turn

Think about a particular interaction with a favorite client, colleague, or boss that brought you great satisfaction. What did this person look like? How, exactly, did the relationship begin? Did she walk into your place of business? Did you meet online? Did you cold-call the client or were you introduced to her? By whom?

Try to remember the details of the story; where were you? What was it like in that room or environment? Were you sitting or standing? Was it raining or sunny? Did the weather play a role in the situation? Think about the conversation itself and try to remember the dialogue. Try to remember details about the client, where she came from, why you ended up together, what was happening in her life, or what happened in her past to create the dynamic with you.

Add whatever details you can into your story portfolio to review later!

Networking

Does that word immediately make you cringe? It doesn't have to. Having a network is critical to your success, and networking is simply the method you use to build your network. That doesn't mean going to every networking event and handing out business cards. It means nurturing relationships in every area of your life. Don't wait until you need an active, supportive network to build one.

Every interaction is an opportunity to build your network. Every phone call at work, every chance encounter at the airport, every time you run into an acquaintance at the grocery store or the bank can create a relationship that becomes part of your network.

It would be impossible to take advantage of every interaction; there are days when we are feeling less than social, less than patient or happy. Those are the days we need to give ourselves some grace, and find activities that won't necessarily involve much interaction with others. Most days, though, as we move through them, offer opportunities for random interactions that can make a difference for you and others.

Think about someone you met on an airplane, or a taxi driver you had a conversation with. Think about someone you met and shared a "small world" story with in a random place. Add a story or two to your story portfolio about those random encounters. Those can be great stories to share when at a networking event, or even with friends.

In-Person Networking Event

No matter your self-identified status of introvert or extrovert, a large networking event can be overwhelming and awkward. It isn't absolutely necessary to participate in this type of event, but they can be a terrific opportunity for exposure of your name, business, and brand.

Rather than force yourself into a position that feels inauthentic or ineffective, use your strengths to come up with a strategy and goals that work for you. If you are comfortable at these events (which is rare), and you love to wander around as a social butterfly, introducing yourself to others, introducing others to each other, and learning just a little bit about each person you meet, make sure you're being strategic about how you're going to follow up with each person.

When I've collected a lot of business cards at an event, as soon as I can discreetly walk away, I jot down notes on the card about the person I met. I might connect immediately with the person on LinkedIn, or use an app on my phone to photograph the card and make notes in the app to remind me of what the person looked like, and any details I can remember about our conversation: kids, dogs, where they grew up, a particular hobby, or something we have in common.

If you're not a rare social butterfly, other strategies can help you succeed in meeting people at this kind of event without feeling overwhelmingly awkward or fake.

In-Person Networking Event, Part 1

I'm pretty comfortable in my skin, but wow, was this an awkward networking event! I didn't know a single person there, and if I hadn't made a big financial investment to attend, I might have walked right back out of that room. I set a goal for myself—and a time limit—so I could live with whatever happened and get out when I needed to. I would introduce myself to five people, do my best to make real connections, and leave in one hour.

The woman made it so easy for me to approach her. Not only did she have a welcoming smile, she was wearing absolutely killer shoes. One thing I know for sure is that when a man or woman wears distinctive shoes, they love to hear about it when you notice them.

"Those shoes!"

"Thanks!" She blushed slightly, obviously just as uncomfortable as I was at that event. "I found them in the back of a vintage clothing store, covered with dust. I couldn't tell if they had ever been worn, and when they fit, I had to have them."

I had to bend down to look at them more closely; the details on the toe were lovely. And as I stood up straight again to ask her what brought her to the event, I noticed two other people moving forward to join us by the high cocktail table near a window.

"What are you looking at?" one man asked.

"Her shoes! They're fantastic." He smiled, looked down at her shoes, and blushed a little. But then I saw him visibly relax as we both smiled back at him. "I love them. My daughter is a huge fan of vintage clothing. Are those vintage, or just made to look that way?"

The woman told the story of finding the shoes, and the newcomers were immediately drawn in.

My friend with the awesome shoes asked, "How old is your daughter? What do you think inspired her to start exploring vintage clothing?"

"When my mother died, I inherited her amazing collection of hats. They're on display on racks in my house, and they're from the '20s, '30s, and the '40s. The only problem I have with them is that we have more to dust. I think that's part of my daughter's interest, that exposure to the collection."

"I love music from those eras! Have you ever heard of Marion Harris, a vocalist who was famous from around 1918 and into the '20s?" I have a tendency to find a way to bring music into almost every conversation. Stories often spark memories of lyrics for me, and I can't help but sing a line or two from a song.

The next time I looked at the time, it was well over an hour later. At some point, at least a dozen people had come through our conversation, introducing themselves and adding their stories along the themes of shoes, parents leaving collections of stuff after they die, children and uncommon interests, and music. I walked away with business cards and stories to go along with them. As soon as I could sit down by myself, I wrote notes on each card to remind me of the story the person shared, or something they mentioned, like the names of their children or their dog or cat adventures.

When I returned home from that event, I followed up with email messages to each of the people I felt I had really connected with, and asked them to keep in touch. A few months later I received a message back from one of them; he hadn't responded to my email and apologized for the delay. Then he asked me for a proposal; he wanted to work with me on his writing and communication.

That contract alone was worth the financial investment I made to attend the event, and he was one person I didn't feel a close connection with at the time. You just never know the impact you might have on a person, and how that will show up later in your life!

It's not difficult to make this magic happen; it's just a matter of being curious and genuinely interested in the wellbeing of the people around you.

Your Turn

Can't find someone approachable with awesome shoes? Look for someone who loves their dog or cat so much that they (accidentally) take them along—you'll see the telltale fur on their coat or skirt. Sometimes the simplest answer is to find the likely commonality that brought you to whatever event you've found yourself attending. Think about something people in your industry have in common, generally, if you're at a work event: Do your peers usually have fur-babies? Are they generally introverts? Do you find a lot of people in your industry like to collect things?

What if you can't look closely at a person, or maybe it's dark? Try finding someone who is smiling awkwardly, and is obviously feeling just as uncomfortable as you are feeling, and ask them what brought them to the event. Or, better yet, ask them if they've read any interesting books or articles lately, seen any live performances, or maybe what they do as a hobby. Ask them anything except "What do you do?" Being able to share something you care more deeply about, rather than a job, is often much more effective in making a person comfortable around you. And when you share a brief story to demonstrate a hobby or interest outside of work, you're likely to draw out a story for the person in front of you, creating a deeper connection.

In-Person Networking Event, Part 2

Walking into the venue for the welcome reception by myself was awkward at best. It was a posh bar, dark, the music was loud, and there was a bowling alley with a handful of lanes. Weird. And coming from a small town in Montana made it even more uncomfortable for me. I hadn't been at a venue like this in many years.

I finally found the one person I knew at the event and beelined for him. He introduced me to the two people he was speaking with, but it was so loud I had a hard time hearing their names. He was heading to the bar and offered to get me a drink. I said yes, and he left me alone with the two people he had introduced me to.

Because of the noise, I was uncomfortable asking the kind of questions I usually rely on to learn about people and connect with them. When my friend returned with drinks, the three of them started to talk over the loud music. I just couldn't get comfortable, so when I finished my drink, I quietly walked away from the group and made my way back to my hotel room.

It felt like a total bust, and I had the painful thought that I might have made a big mistake in investing in attending the conference. None of the people I had met so far had felt real to me, and I started to doubt myself. My confidence was taking a hit.

The next day as the sessions progressed, I decided to make the most of my time there, despite my discomfort about not fitting in with this group. I stood toward the back and made eye contact with the guy running the sound for the microphones. He smiled warmly at me, obviously sensing my awkwardness and relating to it. I suddenly felt so much better; the comfort of sharing that moment brought me out of my funk. For the rest of the day, I focused on meeting the people behind the scenes at the event, and they introduced me to some of the other guests at the conference.

When it was time to make my way to the evening reception, I had found my small community of like-minded people and easily found a place to sit to eat and visit. I had collected a handful of business cards but still didn't feel like I had met anyone I'd choose to keep in touch with. I didn't feel like the event had been worth the investment. I knew my mindset needed to shift so I'd be open to possibility outside of what I had intended or anticipated.

It was within moments of my internal resignation to just find a nugget or two of inspiration or lessons, and then go home and let the experience be whatever it turned out to be, when one of the people I had made jokes with earlier in the day pulled me into a conversation to make an introduction.

The woman he introduced to me had spoken on stage earlier, and her session was a highlight for me that day, one of the few I found relevant and engaging. She hugged me after the introduction, rather than shake my hand, and we immediately launched into an incredible conversation about her session and my takeaways from it.

Not only did I stay in touch with that extraordinary woman, she has been one of my most steadfast supporters and encouragers in my work since then.

Your Turn

When was the last time you went to an event and felt like it was a complete waste of time and money? Did that story trigger a memory for you? What could you have done to shift your mindset at some point during the event?

My strategy was to meet and get to know the event coordinators, the people who were behind the scenes, making the event successful thanks to the tiny details participants never saw. That was my natural instinct because of my experience in event planning, hospitality, and music performance. At any networking event, finding just one person to connect with can be the difference between success and failure at finding value in that kind of investment.

Consider the people in the room you are likely to be able to relate to, maybe the people you can see are also feeling awkward and uncomfortable. I love to use humor to break the ice, making a joke about spilling coffee that morning, or some other self-deprecating remark about feeling awkward.

Adjusting your mindset to be open to any connection and possibility is the critical factor in these situations. If you can shift your perspective, you can always find an opportunity for growth.

Online Networking

I'm a big fan of using LinkedIn and other social networking platforms to build a solid network of supporters, encouragers, clients, and job prospects. It's a great way to intentionally create and build your digital footprint, but it's important to connect and build relationships online in similar ways to how you build them in person.

There are plenty of resources to learn how to build a killer LinkedIn profile; just do a search in your browser. There are also a lot of resources that explain how to make LinkedIn work for you, so I won't go into detail here.

Online networking isn't terribly different from networking in person. If what you are putting online doesn't match what someone would experience with you in person, you're out of alignment, and it's time to be more intentional about your online activities.

On any platform, but especially on LinkedIn, sending a random connection request to someone without a personal note or any context for the reason for the request is unlikely to create a true connection, certainly not an immediate one. Think about it this way:

You're a well-known business owner in your town, standing outside of your building, waiting for your ride. A stranger recognizes you, as you can tell from the expression on his face. He runs up to you, slaps his business card into your hand, and runs away.

You're left standing there, puzzled. You might look at the card, mostly out of curiosity, right? How likely is it that you'll see the business name and have an urge to do business with him? Or how likely is it that you'll see the name on the card and hand it to your hiring manager and let him know this guy would be a perfect hire?

Unlikely, right? Unless he's a comedian, maybe . . .

So, how about this scenario instead:

You're a well-known business owner in your town, standing outside of your building, waiting for your ride. A stranger recognizes you, as you can tell from his expression. He walks up to you, a genuine smile on his face: "Hi, I'm Tom. I recognize you from the newspaper article about your recent recognition for your contribution to the business community here. Thank you for your commitment to our local businesses; I appreciate it. I happen to be one of those business owners who have benefited from your contributions, and I'd love to treat you to a coffee sometime and learn more about what motivates you. Here's my card."

The entire exchange took thirty seconds because as soon as the stranger handed you his business card, he smiled, said "Have a good day!" and walked away. Now, how likely is it that you'll throw away that card without looking at it, or put it into your pocket to add to your collection of thousands of those cards?

There are lots of ways that conversation could go, as long as you acknowledge how you know the person, what caught your attention about them, and your intention for the connection. If you're looking for a job, consider letting the person know you've read about his company and would love to learn more through an informational interview. Is there someone you could contact to set up an appointment with him, or could he introduce you to someone else to interview?

That conversation easily translates to a LinkedIn connection request, but even better than sending a connection request without much context is to actively engage with the person before asking to connect.

Add an insightful comment to the posts of the people who inspire you and who share relevant content. Sharing an article, adding an introduction to explain why you're sharing it, and tagging the original author is a great way to acknowledge your appreciation for their work, and to put yourself on their radar for a future request to connect.

Your Turn

Have you found success in connecting online with potential employers, clients, or colleagues/peers in your industry? Think about how you met someone important to you in your network: Did you reach out to them, or did they reach out to you? How did that first conversation or contact go? Why do you think it did or didn't work?

By adding a few of those stories to your story portfolio, you may identify some key strategies that have worked for you—or with you—in the past, and begin using those strategies more intentionally and strategically.

As you've read through these networking stories, did some of your networking horror and success stories pop into your head? As you add them to your story portfolio, categorize them with your own system based on the likely place you'd share them—interview, job interview, networking event.

"The fact of storytelling hints at a fundamental human unease, hints at human imperfection. Where there is perfection there is no story to tell."

BEN OKRI, POET AND NOVELIST

CHAPTER 8

STORYTELLING: OBSERVATION IS THE KEY

Now that you have the beginning of a story portfolio, it's time to find appropriate places and effective ways to share them! Our best tool for learning to be a great story-sharer is observation. When people tell you stories, pay attention to their body language, facial expressions, and tone of voice. Think about the parts of their storytelling that keep your interest and leave you entertained and eager to listen. Watch for your own reactions to the storyteller: Are you interested and curious? Are you bored or annoyed? Ask yourself what it is about the storytelling that makes you feel the way you feel.

Let's start with the storytelling elements that often go wrong:

- Wrong story for the audience

- Too much detail

- Not enough detail

- Goes on too long

- Not enough emphasis goes into the key point of the story

Wrong Story for the Wrong Audience—Observation

In any conversation, the first thing I do is observe my audience. Whether it is someone I know in the grocery store, or when I'm at the dinner table with my family, I try to be fully present, in the moment, watching the people around me for cues about their mood and current mindset.

It's important to consider observation as a primary tool for storytelling, even when you're speaking to a roomful of strangers. When getting ready for a presentation or workshop, here are some of the observations I use:

Are the majority in the group one gender? Are the majority in the group parents or pet owners?

When I moved to Montana and spent a little time with a "mom's club," the majority of the women in that group were younger than I was and were generally at-home moms. This is the audience for parenting stories, memories of being a kid stories, but probably not career/work/bad boss stories.

Find something interesting about each person: shoes, socks, clothing (is that an old Iron Maiden T-shirt?), hair color/style, purse, jewelry, anything in which you can demonstrate genuine interest, if not compliment.

Look closely at their clothes and posture to find signals of their interests and home life. Is there pet hair you can see? Indications they have children? What about the type of clothes they choose—do they scream fashionista, athlete, outdoorsy, or video-gamer?

There are two primary ways to connect immediately with a person: Find something in common, or find something unique/interesting that you can ask about or compliment.

When you've observed something about a person that you think you might have in common, or something you find interesting, you might find an opportunity to share a brief story about it. Once, when I was feeling particularly awkward when meeting a new colleague, I noticed he had a dog, thanks to the wallpaper image on his phone. I looked down at my slacks and realized I had a few of my dog's hairs on them. I swiped at them and said, "I miss my dog so much when I travel, I often have to take just a bit of him with me!"

That statement immediately opened the door not only for humor, but for sharing stories.

Remember, the intention of sharing a short story is to connect AND to draw out a story from the person in front of you. Some people struggle with finding a story to share, even after you've given them a cue. That's when you start asking questions. You've established that he has a dog, but that's it. You can see from his body language that he's uncomfortable. How? He's shifting his weight from left foot to right foot, he's struggling with eye contact, he keeps moving his hands from in his pockets to out of his pockets; maybe he's even moving just a tiny bit away from you, turning his body slightly.

Asking a few questions with genuine curiosity can shift that discomfort quickly. What kind of dog is it? Did you get him as a puppy, or did you adopt him? What's his name? Does he like to swim or chase sticks? What's your favorite thing to do with him?

Pick a couple of questions to gently encourage him to share. Be ready to share a brief story that might remind him of something he can share about his experience with pets.

Now that you know something about your audience, you can dig into the story portfolio in your head for personal experiences your audience can likely relate to! If you noticed anything pet-oriented or outdoorsy, consider sharing a story of how you ended up with your pet, or how you named it.

With the right audience, I love to share stories of adventures with dogs and kids.

We had two two-person kayaks when our boys were younger, and we took many opportunities to float on the Missouri River between Wolf Creek and Craig, Montana. Setting up and getting there was pretty easy, so easy that we could do it on a summer evening after work. The trip was usually around three hours—a bit faster with wind at our backs, slower with a strong headwind.

We would pack up the dog, the kids, a basic picnic, beer for the adults, and lots of sunscreen, and head up to the river for an afternoon or evening.

On one of these trips, our older son brought his friend, Thomas, and our younger son stayed behind to hang out with Thomas's younger sister at their house. We had our yellow lab, Jaxon, with us. He was an amazing water dog, and incredible swimmer and bird hunter. But he had a major flaw: He hated it when our family was in two separate boats. Jaxon whined nonstop when our boats were too far apart for him to easily protect everyone.

Jacob and Thomas were in one kayak, and we were in the other, the dog sitting in front of me leaning on my legs. As we paddled toward a section of the Missouri with a large island in the middle, Jaxon could see that the boys were going to go one way around, and we were heading toward the other way around. As the two boats got farther from each other, the dog's whining got louder and more insistent.

Jaxon suddenly leaped out of our boat and into the water, gashing my thigh with his sharp nails and strong legs. He swam, whining through his nose, to the other boat. The boys had to pull to the bank of the river to get the dog into their boat, and as we paddled around the far side of the island, we could hear Jaxon's loud, persistent whining until we reconnected at the other end.

Would I share this story in a roomful of executives for a Fortune 500 company? Maybe, but it's much more likely I'd share it when speaking to people in organizations more likely to spend time outdoors, in nature, right? As I look around a room and identify my audience, I can tell pretty quickly if a story of being outside, kayaking with a dog and kids will resonate with them.

Too Much Detail, Too Little Detail, Too Long: Observe Audience Response, Pick Key Points

Usually, my father was a great storyteller, but he was notorious for adding far too much detail to a story, and for a while I followed in his footsteps. On a long drive with him, I noticed that I was vacillating between interest, annoyance, and boredom during one of his stories.

I've always been fascinated by stories and storytelling, and this was a pivot point in my journey toward being a professional storyteller.

In trying to figure out why I was feeling what I was feeling, I started to listen to the elements of his story more closely. He was talking about a project he had taken on at home, a damaged speedboat he had been given by a friend and was starting to fix. My dad told me all about the friend who had given him the boat, how he managed to move the boat from one place to another, the story behind the trailer he now had, all interesting parts to the story. The parts that were making me annoyed or bored were the details about the people involved. He was sharing the names of the friends, their families, kids, cousins, dogs . . . far too much detail, and not at all part of the key points of his story, which was supposed to be about the kindness of the people who were helping him.

When you decide which story to share, based on observations of your audience, pick out the point or theme of the story:

- Is it about the kindness of strangers?
- Is it about your resourcefulness or curiosity?
- What characteristics of yourself and others are you trying to demonstrate through your story, and how do they relate to your audience and the current topic of conversation?

Which details of your story need to be shared in order to truly connect with your audience? The conversation in the car with my father started out with a story I shared about the kindness and generosity of my neighbors. At one point, my dad shared a specific conversation he had with his neighbor's son, who was helping him scrape and paint the boat. That kept my attention; I remember that part of the story, told to me at least ten years ago, because it made sense in the context of our initial conversation.

A few years ago, my brother overheard me trying to share a story with our ten-year-old niece. Trying. That's because she clearly didn't have any interest in the story I was sharing, and at some point, my brother quietly whispered to me, "Sarah, land the plane."

I could easily see my niece wasn't listening, and that my attempt to connect using that particular story wasn't working, so why did I keep talking, adding far more detail to the story than she needed for me to get a point across?

Some of us take a long time to learn certain lessons, and I'm still practicing this one: Cut your losses, land the plane, end the story quickly instead of trying to dig your way out of it. Here's an example:

Our older son was not enjoying seventh grade. I know, we're all shocked that seventh grade was difficult, right?

We tried a few routines in the morning to help him improve his energy and mood on the way to school. Our theme song, blaring through the car on our way, was "Highway to Hell" by AC/DC. Some mornings we'd leave a little early and stop for a donut on the way. But seventh grade is hard for a lot of kids, and no matter what we did, he struggled.

One Monday morning as we buckled our seatbelts, with a smile on his face he said, "Mom, it's going to be a really good week, I just know it!"

It completely surprised me. He was smiling as we drove along, obviously somewhere in his head and humming a song.

"That's terrific! I'm so glad to hear it! So you're going to talk to your math teacher to make sure you get your homework done and turned in this week?"

"Um. Yeah."

"And you'll remember to bring home your gym clothes so I can wash them?"

"Uh huh."

I looked over at him slowly deflating.

"You're right, it's going to be a great week! You are going to have fun with your friends, right?" I went on to share a story about an experience I had in seventh grade, yammering away, trying to dig myself out of this hole.

He was slumped in his seat, barely seeing what was passing outside his window as we drove.

By the time we pulled up to the school and he was getting his backpack on, he was completely deflated. I watched him walk into the school, shoulders slumped.

"Have a good day, sweetie! I love you!"

But the damage was done. I cried all the way to work.

I should have known after the very first "Um. Yeah." But I wasn't paying attention to my audience. I could have stopped there and maybe even asked a question. Instead, I kept digging myself deeper.

Luckily, he has a pretty short attention span for this sort of thing.

When I got to work, I called the school to have him released at lunchtime for a dentist appointment he didn't have. I signed him out, and as we walked to the car, he asked me about it because he didn't remember having an appointment scheduled.

"I just wanted to take you out to lunch. I missed you today!"

We sat down at a local coffee shop with a sandwich and I told him how sad I felt about how things went that morning.

"What do you mean?" was his response. All of the angst from that morning was mine. He was over it almost as soon as he walked through the door of the school.

I was filled with relief, but the lesson wasn't lost on me.

Your Turn

Think about a recent experience when you told a story in which you either went on too long, added far too much detail, lost track of where you were going with it, or one that was the wrong story to share with the wrong person.

Jot down a sentence or phrase to remind you of some details about that experience, where you were, who you were talking to, and the cues you missed at that time.

It's not difficult to gauge a person's response to you and your story. Watch for facial expression and body language in your audience. Is the person looking at you? Are they facing you, or turning away? Watch their feet, if you are standing. Sometimes you can see subtle movement as they step back away from you, and start to turn.

This is probably the most important part of story sharing. If you are losing your audience, don't try to fix the problem by continuing the story or discussion. We all know someone who simply talks a lot, a person we like, but when we're not in the mood and we see them at the grocery store, we walk a little faster and pretend we didn't see them. I know I've been that person. Have you?

Observation of your audience is the key to connecting authentically with them. If you've gone on too long and see the telltale signs of disinterest, lack of curiosity, boredom, defensiveness, anxiety (running late), in the memorable words of my brother, "land the plane."

Use your words:

"I'm sorry, I went off on a tangent. What are you up to today?"

"It looks like you have somewhere to be, so let's catch up another time."

"I get so excited about ___, and I know I'm yammering. How are you doing?"

Public Presentations, Meetings, Professional Events— Prepare for Your Audience

Whether you're speaking in front of four friends, a handful of colleagues, in an interview, or in front of a few hundred people, you can quickly observe certain things about your audience.

Preparation: If you know ahead of time that you're presenting, you can do a little research about your audience. Before I begin to plan a presentation or workshop, I ask the organizers a variety of questions so I am prepared with relevant stories to share. In the case of an interview, I try to find out who will be interviewing me so I can look them up on LinkedIn and find their bios on the website.

Here are some of the questions I might ask or research when preparing for an interview or presentation:

- What will be the gender mix? Will the majority be men or women, or will it be a pretty even distribution?

- Are there different ethnicities and cultures in the room?

- What's the age range of the audience?

- What ties the audience together? Is it their career or industry, their religion, or their hobbies and interests?

- What brings them to your presentation or session? Was it their choice, or a requirement from an employer or family member?

By asking these questions or researching the answers, I can build a picture of my audience. If I have a general idea of the people I'll be speaking with, I'll have a better idea about which stories might be meaningful to them.

Now that you have an idea about which stories to share, based on what you've observed of your audience, it's time to observe their response to you.

If you don't have time to prepare, remember the first part of this chapter. Use your observation skills to quickly determine what your audience needs from you. Stop thinking about yourself, and how you're coming across, and start thinking about what you can bring to your audience. When you know what you bring to the table, you can focus with confidence on your audience and their needs.

Body language is something we often observe in others, sometimes subconsciously, and it's important to observe our own body language to be intentional about how we want to be perceived. There are some great books about public speaking, and one of my favorites is *Talk Like Ted* by Carmine Gallo. Gallo's book focuses on the body language and content of public speakers, offering great guidelines for how and when to move your hands and arms, the pace of your speaking, and general content ideas.

It takes a lot of time and effort to incorporate those guidelines into your speaking! Practice by taking advantage of any opportunities to introduce yourself at a gathering, share an idea in a meeting, facilitate a meeting, or give a presentation to any audience.

No matter how great you think you are doing, the only way to tell whether your points are being made, and you're being perceived as you intend, is to observe your audience.

When I gave a presentation at a Women's Leadership Network of Helena meeting, my friend Tammy Copenhaver offered the best indication of an engaging, inspiring presentation when I asked her how she thought it went.

"I always watch participants for how many times they pick up their pens. I lost count during your presentation, so I think it went really well."

What other cues can you use to determine whether you're engaging and connecting with your audience?

You're standing up in a meeting with a handful of colleagues, and you must present your idea in a compelling way. You know your audience, and you've selected just the right personal story to share to begin the proposal. As you're speaking, you notice two of your colleagues slowly lean back in their chairs, crossing their arms in front of their chests. What can you tell by that movement? Can you adjust your presentation to win them back?

If more than one person leans back and crosses their arms, you likely said something that either made them uncomfortable (which is okay sometimes, if they need to consider something that conflicts with their ideas), insulted, or they're cold.

In most cases, you can ask one of them if what you said made them uncomfortable, or if they felt you insulted them. If you can open the door to that discussion, you may be able to pull a story from them to help you understand why they feel the way they do.

If you don't feel comfortable asking direct questions, ask your audience questions about their experience with the topics and concepts you're describing. Help them tell their stories by asking for specific details about where they were, who was involved, and how they were feeling at the time. Be curious. And try hard not to be defensive in that moment! It's easy to feel personally insulted in this scenario. Remember the personal brand exercise in the beginning of the book? Consider those words again, in the context of this situation. Are you demonstrating the qualities and values you intend to demonstrate?

You've heard the phrase "You can't please everyone." And that's absolutely true. There will always be people in the audience that don't find your presentation relevant or particularly engaging. It's important to observe the body language of the majority of your audience and not to focus too much on one person with her arms crossed on her chest.

One thing I've learned after hundreds of presentations and performances is that you really cannot know what your audience is thinking and experiencing. The presentations that felt like the biggest flops at the time often turned out to be the most successful in the long run, thanks to referrals and post-conference conversation follow-ups.

"Analogies, it is true, decide nothing, but they can make one feel more at home."

SIGMUND FREUD

CONCLUSION: AN ANALOGY

S tories connect us. They help us relate to each other and deepen our understanding of experiences in our lives. Analogies can give us an entirely different perspective and help us create a more visual representation of emotional experiences.

I love a good analogy; I can share a story of an experience I had, but if the audience hasn't had a similar experience, they may not be able to relate to it.

I wrote the following analogy to help me put things in perspective when I was having a hard time in a job that was not only a bad fit for me and my skills; it was a job that I allowed to sink my confidence and health. Each time I reread it, I am reminded to think about where I am, where I want to be, and how I want to get there.

When I was at the end of my patience with that job, I reached out to a few mentors for help. I asked one friend to visit with me and provide ideas and guidance; I hoped for concrete advice. What I got was not at all what I had envisioned, and as I walked out of her office, I thought it had been a waste of my lunch break.

Lucky for me, the year had been one of tremendous growth, personally and professionally, so instead of leaving my thoughts there, I realized there had to be a reason I went seeking her guidance. I knew there must have been something in the conversation I could use and absorb into my experiences. I was right. What she gave me was the beginning of an analogy I've tossed and turned in my head—and continue to reinvent to serve different situations.

"Sometimes I feel like I'm in my car on the highway, stuck behind a big truck, a car carrier. I look up at the end car on that truck and pray it doesn't fall off the trailer onto my head."

For months I've been driving my car along the highway, stuck behind a big truck. Because I have a tendency toward being impulsive (don't laugh), I have been driving very close to the back of the truck. I have been so incredibly frustrated being stuck here, so I keep swerving out to check for an opportunity to pass the truck, only to find a blind curve or a line of vehicles coming toward me, so I swerve back behind the truck, more and more angry and impatient.

Not only am I angry and frustrated and feeling all the muscles and tendons in my neck getting more painful and stiff, I'm making everyone else in the car uncomfortable. I'm driving so close to the truck that I can't see anything I'm passing outside the car; the beautiful landscapes I'm driving through are lost to me. All I can see is the dust and debris the truck is kicking up into my windshield, and I'm breathing the fumes coming out the back. I'm missing the music playing on my radio and the conversations going on in the back seat, conversations that are precious and unlikely to happen again.

I'm driving so close that the inexperienced (and mean) truck driver is driving even more erratically, making significant and dangerous errors because he is watching my car come so close.

I have choices to make. I can keep swerving to check whether I have an opportunity to pass, not really caring whether the opportunity takes me toward a positive destination, or I can sit back in my seat and get a little space between me and the back of the truck. I can keep being frustrated and sometimes angry at that damn truck in front of me, or I can make some space between us so I can see opportunities from a distance and gauge whether they might be right for me and my passengers. I can choose to see the truck much more clearly by giving it room so I can learn more about it and be able to avoid trouble, and maybe even help if necessary. I'm not in denial; I know the truck will cloud my view here and there, kicking up big gusts and clouds of snow and rain, and that I won't always be able to keep from getting frustrated. But with the space I'm creating between me and the truck, I can at least try to enjoy the music, the view, and the passengers in my car.

Eventually, that truck is going to get off the highway, or I'm going to find a good opportunity to pass. I can't get off the highway at the next exit because there are people in the car that are relying on me to keep on truckin', so to speak. And as one of my dearest friends said, "You have great company in the car!"

My sister would say that I have always lived my life knowing that it is not about the destination, but about the journey . . . So here I am, driving my car and (usually) making better choices, enjoying the view, including some interesting and sometimes dangerous and frustrating weather. I'll keep on driving behind the truck until I find the right opportunity for me and my passengers. I'll continue to be grateful for the comfort of my friends and family traveling with me, and I'll most definitely sit back and enjoy the music.

What's your truck right now? Have there been bigger trucks in your way? How will you handle the next slow-moving truck you're stuck behind?

Your Turn

You've read analogies that made you think more deeply about an experience, right? Consider different aspects of your life-pivot stories; think about how those pivot points can be associated with travel via train, car, plane, etc. Maybe one of your life-pivot stories can be considered in terms of something in nature—a storm, snow, rain, sunny weather. Listening to music often puts me into a place where I relate the lyrics to some part of my life; "Ain't No Sunshine" or "Sunny Side of the Street" are examples.

WORKING THROUGH YOUR
STORY PORTFOLIO

Throughout this book, I've asked you to consider the points in your life that changed or confirmed your path. They may involve marriage, divorce, children, death, a traumatic event, or something subtler, like a random comment from a stranger or mentor. Being able to share two or three of these stories offers a glimpse for others into how you think. The pivot points in your life are generally a point of vulnerability, when you had to put yourself into an uncomfortable place and take risks you normally wouldn't take.

Life pivots are the foundation of our identity. If you can pick out a handful of experiences that really changed the way you think, and tell those stories convincingly, the results are powerful. How many rags-to-riches stories have we read over the years? What is the actual part that stands out in those stories? The call to action. The part that resonates with readers and audiences is the pivot point in the story, the point at which the narrator says, "This is what happened that made me realize. . ." or "This is what happened that made me take action, the thing that made me take the leap."

Audiences need to see some aspect of vulnerability in order to feel emotionally engaged with you and your story. Offer that glimpse into your humanity by sharing part of your history that changed you.

Think about these things as you craft your stories with details:

1. Who is your audience, and why should your audience care about your point?

2. What do you want your audience to do or feel?

3. Provide details about the context of the situation and the people involved.

4. Provide a specific action you took to solve a problem.

5. Describe the other people in the situation who were affected and/or involved in the solution (teamwork, credit where credit is due).

6. Provide a clear indication of how the story ends (the accomplishment and its effect on you, the customer, and the organization).

How many times have you been in a group, trying to make a clear point and struggling with getting people to understand? This happens a lot, particularly when someone feels really passionate about an issue and feels the need to defend their answers.

Take the time to build your story portfolio, clearly identifying the lessons in each story, the moment in the story that you want to capture your audience's attention, curiosity, and imagination. When the time comes—and it will—and you hear "Tell me about yourself," you'll be *ready*.

"The universe is made of stories, not of atoms."

MURIEL RUKEYSER

ROCK STAR MOMENTS
WORKSHEET

Rock Star Moments/Satisfaction Journal
(Specific Moments or experiences that brought you great satisfaction)

STORY PORTFOLIO
WORKSHEETS

	Era 1: *(Example: Seventh Grade)*
Story 1	
Story 2	
Story 3	
Story 4	
Story 5	

	Era 2:
Story 1	
Story 2	
Story 3	
Story 4	
Story 5	

	Era 3:
Story 1	
Story 2	
Story 3	
Story 4	
Story 5	

	Era 4:
Story 1	
Story 2	
Story 3	
Story 4	
Story 5	

	Era 5:
Story 1	
Story 2	
Story 3	
Story 4	
Story 5	

	Interview Stories
Story 1	
Story 2	
Story 3	
Story 4	
Story 5	

	Small World/Networking Stories
Story 1	
Story 2	
Story 3	
Story 4	
Story 5	

	Career Pivot Stories
Story 1	
Story 2	
Story 3	
Story 4	
Story 5	

A NOTE FROM THE AUTHOR

April 2020

I finished writing this book in November 2019, just a few months prior to the COVID-19 pandemic, with absolutely no idea how 2020 would transform our global community. In a very short period of time, thousands lost their lives, millions lost their jobs and businesses, families were pulled apart and quarantined together, and the global economy realized how tightly connected we really are. As communities, we saw healthcare workers sainted, bullied, and celebrated when entire cities howled like wolves during shift changes to recognize them for the risks they were taking to care for our sick.

Meanwhile, many of us hunkered down to shelter in place, faced with daily uncertainty of our health, our jobs, school closures, and being barraged with moment-by-moment shifts in the news about the short and long-term impacts of this pandemic.

People have found ways to cope, of course, and there have been beautiful stories of families reconnecting and spending quality time together making meals, taking walks, and reading together.

For me, a huge fiftieth birthday celebration was planned for April 18, 2020, complete with friends and family coming to Montana from all over the country. It didn't happen, of course. What happened instead was a gorgeous hike with a friend—with appropriate social distancing, a virtual wine tasting, a brief paddle around in a nearby lake with a new kayak, some heartfelt, amazing video birthday messages, a surprise Zoom birthday toast with friends from all over the world, including Australia, and a Facebook Live performance of a few songs by me and my husband, Bob.

When I had time to think about the events of the weekend, I found them truly inspiring. And while I was disappointed not to celebrate the way I intended, the stories we created together for this big birthday were probably more significant, more life-altering than if things had gone the way we planned. Instead of focusing on the disappointment, I lived each experience in the reality of the moment.

Some have called this time "The Great Pause." One friend described his bike ride in a city north of London: "I could have ridden on either side of the street, it was so deserted. And the air. The air was crisp and fresh; I've never smelled it like this here."

That's what this book is about, really—seeing that the stories of the things that happen in our lives are significant, far more than the things that *didn't* happen in our lives.

I have great empathy for the students and young adults whose lives were so disrupted in their final year of school. I cannot imagine the depth of disappointment in missing the major experiences they were expecting to have: prom, graduation, parties, goodbyes, all of those "this is the last time . . ." moments. Those disappointments feel so big right now, and I can tell you they will pale in comparison to the adventures that await you.

Please take time now to begin collecting stories of this experience, to remember the details of incidents and situations that you can look back at, to see how pivotal they were in how you see yourself and how you see your future. Consider the tragic loss of life, and the courageous acts of our healthcare and service workers, and also the smaller acts that made a difference, like the many who took up the call to sew masks for themselves and others, and neighbors delivering food to each other. Reflect on your stories of this time in the context of the stories of the people around you.

You've heard people ask each other: "Where were you on 9/11?" "Do you remember what you were doing when you heard the news about . . . ?"

In the future, people will ask you those questions about your time during the COVID-19 pandemic. I hope that as you think about your experiences during this time, you begin to collect details of some specific moments, conversations, walks, time you spent with your kids, your partner, your fur babies, in the kitchen, or on video calls. Take time periodically to jot down notes about your day, the way you were feeling, your thoughts, and how you spent your precious days.

This is the time, my friends, to consider the stories you will share in the future, because YOUR stories, the ones you make right now, are what will give our collective future meaning, and will give context to the suffering, joy, and transformation we will see as a result of those experiences.

Do not waste this opportunity. Because it's not what happens to you that shapes your identity and your relationships. It's how you talk about it.

ACKNOWLEDGMENTS

I knew writing a book would be a challenge, that demonstrating this level of vulnerability would be intense. Handing over the first draft to my editor, Susan Rooks, was like the first time you hire a babysitter for your newborn baby. She knew her first response would be powerful, for better or worse, in my book-writing journey. I am so grateful for her initial response, and her help in making me look and sound as smart as I can. "It's good. (And there is no 'but' . . . you were waiting for a 'but,' right?)"

Thank you to my biggest cheerleader, the one who believes in me, while asking the tough questions to help me move forward with some degree of preparation. I always feel loved and supported by my husband, Bob. He is a role model for our fabulous boys, Jacob and Max, who inspire me daily with their compassion, kindness, and intelligence.

My father kept me company as I wrote this book, my memories of him are so vivid, and he continues to be an important part of my storytelling journey. I miss him every day.

I'm grateful for the support of my mother, Ruth Elkins, and the extraordinary relationship I share with my siblings, Karen Elkins Cohen and Eric Elkins, that has sustained and inspired me through many life and career transformations.

To my LinkedIn community and the No Longer Virtual tribe, thank you for your unending support and encouragement. I wouldn't have even considered taking this step without you.

This book would not have happened without the encouragement and assistance from my dear friend Neil Hughes. It's because of him the *Your Stories Don't Define You* podcast exists, and became the inspiration for this book.

CPSIA information can be obtained
at www.ICGtesting.com
Printed in the USA
LVHW051312020720
659500LV00007B/483